W9-BEK-542

GENGHIS KHAN

MILITARY PROFILES

SERIES EDITOR

Dennis E. Showalter, Ph.D.

Colorado College

Instructive summaries for general and expert readers alike, volumes in the Military Profiles series are essential treatments of significant and popular military figures drawn from world history, ancient times through the present.

GENGHIS KHAN

History's Greatest Empire Builder

Paul Lococo, Jr.

Potomac Books, Inc.
Washington, D.C.

Library of Congress Cataloging-in-Publication Data

Lococo, Paul, 1954–
  Genghis Khan : history's greatest empire builder / Paul Lococo, Jr.
      p. cm. — (Military profiles)
  Includes bibliographical references and index.
  ISBN-13: 978-1-57488-571-2 (hardcover : alk. paper)
  ISBN-13: 978-1-57488-746-4 (pbk. : alk. paper)
  1. Genghis Khan, 1162–1227. 2. Mongols—Kings and rulers—
Biography. 3. Conquerors—Asia—Biography. I. Title.
  DS22.L6 2008
  950'.21092—dc22

                        2007035674

Printed in the United States of America on acid-free paper that meets the
American National Standards Institute Z39-48 Standard.

Potomac Books, Inc.
22841 Quicksilver Drive
Dulles, Virginia 20166

First Edition

10 9 8 7 6 5 4 3 2 1

Contents

> *O people, know that you have committed great sins, and*
> *that the great ones among you have committed these sins. If*
> *you ask me what proof I have for these words, I say it is*
> *because I am the punishment of God. If you had not com-*
> *mitted great sins, God would not have sent a punishment*
> *like me upon you.*[1]

In June 1219 Genghis Khan led his army to attack the city of Bukhara, one of the major Muslim cities in Central Asia and part of the Khwarazm Empire. The attack by the Mongols was unexpected—something Genghis Khan had counted on—but twenty thousand defenders left the city to confront the Mongols. With the defenders defeated amid much slaughter, Bukhara's leading men came out to offer the surrender of the city. After seeing to the feeding of his men and ordering the population to leave the city, Genghis Khan had the city's leaders gather at the main mosque. It was there that he delivered his "sermon" on the reasons for the disaster that had befallen the city.

Genghis Khan was not merely a brutal, bloodthirsty barbarian. As his proclamation to Bukhara's elders, which begins this preface, demonstrates, Genghis Khan took care to understand his enemies and was ready to use not only warfare but also propaganda, appeals to economic self-interest, and even diplomacy to achieve his aims of domination and conquest. But let there be no mistake, battle was the primary tool for this conqueror.

It was through his bitter experience growing up on the steppes of Mongolia that Genghis Khan learned to trust very few people and to be constantly aware of the people and events around him. As a result of an early life filled with hardship, betrayals, and constant struggle, Genghis Khan developed into a cunning and effective leader of men in battle. He became a leader who was innovative, and he disdained customary military tactics when those tactics did not serve to bring victory. Once he united the tribes of Mongolia in a way never before seen on the steppes, Genghis Khan led them to almost superhuman victories over forces vastly larger than their own. By the time of his death he had created an empire of immense proportions, larger than anything before in history.

This book aims to help explain how the teenage son of a minor Mongol chieftain created a military machine of extraordinary striking power and wielded that power to defeat and conquer such lands as China, Central Asia, and Persia. This is not a full biography of the world conqueror, but instead focuses on his early struggles to survive, his unification of the Mongolian tribes, and finally his campaigns of conquest. Little will be said about subjects such as how Genghis Khan set up administration of conquered territories or his personal relations with family and friends.

I would like to thank Rick Russell, the editor at Potomac Books who saw me through the process of writing this book and whose patience deserves a medal. Among those who helped me with advice and counsel as I completed the early drafts, I want to especially thank David French. My wife Katherine deserves tremendous credit for her support and advice, not the least of which was suggesting that I take a trip to the Mongolian grasslands to see for myself where Genghis Khan launched his first invasion of China.

Chronology

Mongolian Background

THE CLIMATE and geography of the Mongolian steppe lands are very harsh, and those who survived in such an environment grew up to be hardy and strong. The area produced tough survivors who rose out of a necessarily small population. The steppes of Inner Asia cover a vast amount of the heart of the northern hemisphere, ranging from Hungary to Manchuria. Winter is a time of biting cold when the lands are frozen. Spring brings a period of quite a bit of rain that leaves a carpet of green, with lots of flowers but few trees. The fierce heat of summer in July and August burns off most of this green carpet, and then for a few weeks in the autumn the rains return. Winter cold begins in October, and by November usually all streams and rivers are frozen. It is usual for summer temperatures to reach over 100 degrees Fahrenheit and for winter temperatures to dip to –44 degrees. Throughout the year, depending on the season, Mongolia is subject to thunderstorms, snowstorms, and sandstorms.

To the west Mongolia sees the Altai and Tianshan mountain ranges. In its south, the steppe lands run into the sandy, forbidding Gobi Desert, the source of most of the sand whipped up by the winds. To the north lie the Siberian forests, habitat of some of the forest-dwelling Mongolian tribes and believed by some to be the original homeland of all Mongolian tribes. Mongolia itself lies on a plateau and a few smaller mountain ranges such as the Sayan, Hangay, Yablonoy, and Greater Khingan ranges, lie within its boundaries. Many of the mountains are lush with vegetation, and many times the ranges served as a refuge for defeated Mongol clans, horses, and flocks. In contrast to the mountainous regions, the Mongolian steppes have often been described as "monotonous," with a vast expanse of flat land and very few ravines or hills.

The first Mongols came down from Siberia and eventually settled in the area of present-day Outer Mongolia. Most of the Mongol tribes settled in the region between the Onon and Kerulen rivers, tributaries of the Amur River. Mongolian legends say that in the ninth century the then-leader of the tribes, called Bodonchar, chose this spot because of its fertility, the location's protection from attack by other steppe tribes, and its placement far enough away from China to make invasion from that quarter very unlikely, if not impossible.

In fact, very little beyond legends is known of Mongols before Genghis Khan. By the twelfth century, the Mongol tribes could be divided into two main groups: pastoral nomads and forest hunters. The pastoral nomads raised cattle, sheep, goats, and horses and also engaged in hunting. Their main hunting weapons were arrows and lassoes. At the end of every autumn, most animals were usually slaughtered and their meat frozen, for the fodder for animals would soon become scarce. The pastoral tribes moved several times a year, and location of fodder was the key to their movements. The seasonal scarcity of fodder also led to frequent fighting with other steppe tribes who also relocated, attempting to do the same thing.

Most of the Mongol tribes practiced a form of shamanism in which mediums, often women, formed a mystic union with the spirit world that dominated so much of life. These mediums could relay the concerns of the spirits and even bargain with them for assistance in this world. It has been claimed that some mediums had the ability to control the spirits through the use of certain incantations, smoke, and herbs. Ruling above all spirits was Tengri, or Heaven, the great spirit that protected the Mongols. Before launching any expedition, Genghis Khan prayed to Tengri for success, and he eventually came to believe that Tengri had chosen him to create a large empire.

The Mongols were one of many Altaic peoples—peoples with similar linguistic links—inhabiting the steppe lands. Since at least the ninth century most of the tribes living in Mongolia spoke related languages, mostly of Turkic origin, or archaic Mongolian.[1] Even those, such as the Tatars, who were not directly related to the Mongols, spoke a dialect understood by all in the region. In fact, until the Mongol conquests, it was common for the tribes, including the Mongols, to refer to themselves and their language as "Tatar," not Mongol.[2] By the middle of the thirteenth century, the dominance of the Mongols was so complete that all the peoples and their languages were referred to simply as Mongolian. It has also been customary to describe the whole region as Mongolia, including areas not traditionally inhabited by the Mongols but by groups that shared their steppe-nomadic lifestyle.

The Mongols themselves were divided into tribes and clans with several subclans. In general, an individual's primary loyalty and daily contact was with the clan or, more often, the subclan. Chiefs of subclans often dominated unless there was a particularly charismatic or forceful clan or tribal chief. By tradition, one had to marry outside of the clan. The wife would join her husband's family and thus his clan and tribe. Polygamy was very common, and the first wife had a higher status compared with later wives, though a husband could and often did pick a later wife to hold the title of First Wife. Because of the need to obtain wives from outside the clan, abduction of women was one very common purpose of Mongol raiding, and these abductions were also often the cause of wars. In addition, the youngest son of the First Wife inherited his father's estate.

Prior to and during the wars of unification in the late twelfth century the Mongol tribe was itself divided into two major clans: Borjigin and Taijiut. The Borjigin, Genghis Khan's tribe, were pastoral nomads and settled between the Onon and Kerulen rivers. The Taijiut clan included both pastoral and forest subclans and lived primarily along the Onon River where it flows toward the forestland to the north.

Other powerful Mongol tribes in the twelfth century were the Kereit and the Naiman. The Kereit were Turkish and practiced Nestorianism, a branch of Christianity with origins in Persia, but most of its followers were located in Central Asia. The Naiman were very much under Uighur influence and also followed Nestorian Christianity. One scholar of the

Mongolian peoples believes the Naiman were essentially "Mongolicized Turks."[3] A forest tribe of Mongols named Oirat settled west of Lake Baikal and was among the last of the steppe peoples to be conquered by Genghis Khan. Eventually this tribe became the dominant Mongol tribe during the Ming period (1368–1644) and claimed to be continuing the great enterprise of Genghis Khan.

Other, non-Mongol but powerful tribes in Mongolia included the Merkit and the Tatars. The Merkit were a forest tribe and strong antagonists to the Mongols of Genghis Khan's subclan. The Tatars were another strong opponent of the Mongols, though they spoke a Mongol language. The Tatar homelands were established mostly by Lake Buyur and Lake Kolun and near the Khingan Mountains. The Tatars had an especially fierce reputation. They often came into opposition with or were co-opted by Jin China. The Chinese of the time often referred to all Mongol speakers as "Tatar." Even Europeans often referred to Mongols as Tatars. Later, this was influenced by the Latin name "Tartarus," and thus Europeans often called the Mongols "Tartars," or soldiers from Hell. The Kirghiz were another Turkish tribe that came to join the Mongols after their conquest by Genghis Khan. They had been powerful in the ninth century and had formed a large empire, but in the tenth century, the Khitans, a group of forest tribes from Manchuria, drove them out of Mongolia.

The many tribes and clans in Mongolia fought each other almost constantly over grazing lands, flocks, women, or other treasures they might possess. It was not always a battle of all against all, however, and alliances were common, even if just as commonly broken. Larger alliances of convenience were sometimes formed in order to plunder northern China or some of the oasis towns and cities of Turkistan. As sometimes happened in the steppe lands, one powerful individual managed to create a large confederation of many of the tribes. This was not at all easy and took an individual skilled in battle, diplomacy, steppe politics, character assessment, and treachery to succeed.

According to legend the Mongol people were descended from the union of a grey wolf (a hunter) and either a human female or a tawny doe. After several generations (or, as it was dated then, eight generations before Genghis Khan), a Mongol woman named Alan-goa gave birth to a son, named Bodonchar, years after her husband had died. She claimed a "golden man" who came from the heavens to visit her at night had impregnated her.[4] Apparently, her people accepted this explanation—though her earlier, "legitimate" sons continued to harbor doubts—as she further related that this golden man informed her that the descendants of Bodonchar would eventually come to conquer and rule the whole world. Bodonchar is also credited with being the founder of the Borjigin tribe and the direct ancestor of Genghis Khan.[5]

In the mid-1100s one Bodonchar descendant named Kabul Khan became leader of the Mongols and, for a while, unified a major portion of Mongolia. (This was a loose federation and should not be confused with the true centralized unification achieved in the late twelfth century by Genghis Khan.)

In order to keep the tribes' allegiance, Kabul Khan raided northern China, taking advantage of China's preoccupation with another war. Song dynasty China (916–1127) had formed an unwise alliance with a Manchurian forest-dwelling people called Jurchen. The Song Chinese hoped this alliance would help them recover an expanse of Chinese territory around the area of the present-day city of Nanjing that at that time was occupied by another Manchurian people, the Khitan. The enormous infantry armies of the Chinese were repulsed time and again by the Khitan's primarily cavalry forces. The Song Chinese expected that with the Jurchen cavalry attacking from the north and the Chinese infantry from the south and west, the Khitan would be defeated. After victory the Jurchens were to gain control of the Khitan lands in Manchuria, with the Chinese recovering their lost territories. The combined assault took place in 1124, yet once again, the Khitan repulsed the Chinese attacks. However, the Jurchen attacks not only succeeded in destroying the Khitan forces, but also continued farther into China. Within a year, Chinese armies had been forced south of the Yellow River, and the imperial court fled south as well. Wars between the Jurchen and the Chinese continued for years, but by 1127 the Jurchen had set up a Chinese-style government in the north they called the Jin (or "Gold") dynasty (1115–1234), and the Chinese reorganized the now "Southern" Song dynasty (1127–1279), with a "temporary" capital at Hangzhou.

It was this division of China into two competing and warring dynasties that Kabul Khan took advantage of when he launched his raids in 1135. To keep the Jin rulers from shifting their full attention to the north, Kabul Khan did accept a nominal relationship as a tributary.

The Jin emperor sent an emissary to demand Kabul Khan appear and prostrate himself before the emperor. In a drunken rage at this arrogance of the Jin, Kabul Khan killed the emissary. The Jin next sent a small expedition against the Mongol federation, but this, too, was defeated. In 1139 the two sides signed a peace treaty and Kabul Khan was designated the "King of the Mongols." He went on to successfully lead a joint expedition with the Jin to crush the Tatars, a tribe not part of the Mongol federation. The Jin, like all Chinese dynasties, were very wary of any strong grouping in Mongolia, so after Kabul Khan's natural death they secretly allied with the Tatars to strike against the Mongols. Their task was made much easier since several Mongol tribes dropped out of the federation upon Kabul Khan's death. Kabul Khan's successor, his brother Ambakai, while a skillful warrior and political operator himself, was hard-pressed to maintain what unity remained. Battles with the Tatars were almost constant until both sides negotiated a peace treaty in 1147. To seal the treaty, the Tatars proposed a marriage of Ambakai to a Tatar princess. When Ambakai and a small retinue arrived for the marriage ceremony, they were taken prisoner and delivered to the Jin in China. There Ambakai and Bodonchar's eldest son were strapped to wooden donkeys and executed. Genghis Khan learned this story of betrayal by both the Tatars and the Jin early in his childhood, and he retained a burning ambition to avenge this deceit. In fact, Genghis Khan later cited the death of Ambakai as his reason for attacking China.

However, revenge had to wait. By the time of Genghis Khan's birth the Mongol tribes were scattered and disorganized. Many years and one more Tatar atrocity had to occur before Genghis Khan could enact vengeance.

The Early Years

LEGENDS, AND SOME passages in the *Secret History of the Mongols*, say that during his life Genghis Khan feared only three things: his mother, his wife, and dogs.[1] We will discuss his wife later on, but there can be no doubt that Genghis Khan's mother was a formidable woman. Her strength of will and character were clear from the time she entered history in the mid-twelfth century.

Hoelun—the future mother of the world conqueror—was a member of the Onggirat clan and married a leader of a clan of the Merkit tribe sometime in 1164. At the time, the Merkits were one of the two dominant non-Mongol tribes (along with the Tatars) in Mongolia. As Hoelun traveled by cart with her new husband back to his territory in the Merkit lands, the party was spotted by Yesügei, leader of the Kiryat subclan of the Borjigin clan of the Mongol tribe, who allegedly was struck by her beauty. Yesügei rushed back to his camp and, with the help of two of his brothers, raced back to capture the beautiful woman. Seeing the three men charging toward them, Hoelun told her husband to escape and leave her. If they were never to see each other again, she told him to think of her and give her name to a future wife. When Yesügei and his brothers arrived to capture her, she resisted, and her screams "raised waves on the river and shook trees in the valley."[2] In earlier times, this sort of forcible assault on a newlywed couple would have been unusual, but in the unsettled times of the twelfth century, it had become increasingly common. Hoelun informed Yesügei that her husband had escaped, but otherwise she accepted her fate and was married to him soon after. With her marriage to Yesügei complete she displayed strong loyalty to her new husband, one time helping him escape an ambush. She also gave birth to four sons—Temüjin, Qasar, Qachiun, and Temüge—and one daughter—Tamülün.

The oldest, Temüjin, was born in 1165 with a clot of blood in his small fist. This, according to Mongol legend, presaged his glorious future. Yesügei gave the future Genghis Khan the name Temüjin, after a Tatar leader Yesügei killed in battle. Many Mongols believed the spiritual power of a defeated enemy might transfer to the victor, and Yesügei may have been attempting to give that power to his newborn son. Or, it might have been an example of Yesügei's well-known vainglory. Whatever the truth, the root of the name is "iron," making young Temüjin a "man of iron."

Temüjin's early years were mostly spent with his nomadic tribe on the upper reaches of the Onon and Kerulen rivers. The Mongol tribes and clans fought each other often in those early years, as various leaders struggled to gain supremacy or at least to lead a major confederation or alliance. When Temüjin was about nine years old, Yesügei decided to find a bride for his oldest son. This decision meant Temüjin's life was about to take a completely unexpected turn.

While making the rounds of friendly clans in search of a wife for Temüjin, Yesügei stopped in at the camp of Hoelun's tribe, the Onggirat. At dinner, the Onggirat leader, Dai Sechen, watched as Temüjin did serious damage to a large bone and a bowl of kumis. To Yesügei he said, "Your son, Temüjin, has fire in his eyes and a bright power in his face," and suggested a marriage to his daughter, Börte, then ten.[3] Yesügei agreed and the two settled the arrangements that night. They decided that Temüjin would live with the Onggirat until he was in his early teens and old enough to marry. And so, the future Genghis Khan came to meet the second person of whom he was afraid.[4]

As Yesügei rode home he ran into a party of Tatars. They seemed friendly and invited him to join them for a meal. Having fought often against the Tatar tribe, Yesügei was hesitant, but he stayed awhile and the meal and friendly conversation relaxed him. After leaving the Tatar camp, Yesügei had not traveled very far when he began to take ill. The Tatars had poisoned him. By the time he reached home he was on his deathbed, and he sent out a servant to go back to the Onggirat and fetch Temüjin. However, Temüjin did not arrive home in time to see his father alive.

Yesügei's death marked the beginning of a very harsh time for Temüjin and his family, but it hardened him to the realities of life in Mongolia at that time. He was abandoned by most of his tribe, for they wanted older, more experienced leadership. For all intents and purposes, the Kiryat subclan would disappear, but Temüjin's experiences over the next few years not only taught him how to survive but also how to take advantage of his situation to create a new reality on the steppes.

Many members of the Kiryat clan left his camp soon after the mourning ceremonies for Yesügei were over. Temüjin was confused and asked his mother for help. Hoelun at one point rode out and forced one group comprised of nearly half the clan to stop and listen to her pleas for unity. This was to no avail, and within less than a year, all the families of the clan had departed, leaving Temüjin with his mother, brothers, sister, a few servants, and two half-brothers by another one of Yesügei's wives. Hoelun kept the group together and taught them how to survive. Hoelun moved her small band to marginal pasturelands where they remained for the next couple of years. She knew here they would face fewer enemies, and, if they could survive the elements, there would be a chance for her children to grow older, stronger, and wiser.

Her efforts were made especially difficult since the sons of different mothers did not get along. She was unable to convince them that unity was essential to their survival, and the conflicts just increased as time passed. One time Temüjin shot a lark, which was forcibly taken from him by his two half-brothers. A few days later, Temüjin and his brother Qasar caught a fish in a stream, which was also promptly taken by their half-brothers. When the two went to Hoelun for help, she merely admonished them all to get along. This would not do for Temüjin, so he and Qasar ambushed one of their half-brothers and shot and killed him with arrows. He died calmly, asking that the remaining half-brother be allowed to live, a request that was granted. Hoelun was furious and scolded Temüjin, baffled as to why he would make their small group even smaller. But Temüjin's slaying of his half-brother was more than merely an example of youthful petulance or unrestrained rage at an insult. The killing was not a sudden act of passion; Temüjin carefully planned and carried out the execution of his half-brother. In this act Temüjin displayed a character trait that would later lead him to totally remake Mongol society. He ruthlessly crushed challenges to his authority, and no Mongol custom or tradition would be allowed to stand in his way.

As a small boy Temüjin had made friends with a young Jadirat boy named Jamuga. They were nearly inseparable, and before Yesügei was killed they had formed an *anda*, or blood brother, relationship. The Mongol anda relationship was a means by which men not related by blood, clan, or tribe could form a close bond. Normally there was a ceremony in which the two anda drank kumis mixed with a small amount of each other's blood in front of witnesses. The sight of two small boys performing an anda ceremony apparently provoked a great deal of laughter from the adults who witnessed it. Although forming such a bond was unusual for small children, the two took the friendship seriously and they remained close for several years, even after Jamuga returned to his tribe.

At age fifteen the whole adventure of life nearly came to a premature end for Temüjin. One of the subclans that had accepted Yesügei's authority was the Taichiut. After Yesügei's death, the Taichiut left the encampment. After several years passed, their leader became concerned that when the children of Yesügei grew up they would nurture a grievance and seek vengeance, a not unreasonable assumption. He therefore determined to attack the children before they got much older. In the attack Hoelun and most of the camp escaped, but Temüjin was captured. For some reason not mentioned in such records as *The Secret History of the Mongols*, Temüjin was not killed but instead was made a slave of the Taichiut who forced him to live with a heavy and humiliating cangue around his neck. A cangue is a wooden yoke with an opening for the head—and sometimes the hands— that is placed around the neck and on the shoulders. The use of cangues was a very common form of punishment in China and some parts of Inner Asia. Temüjin was able to escape with the help of one sympathetic member of the clan. Word of this escape later greatly enhanced Temüjin's reputation among the Mongols, regardless of clan or tribe.

The following year, with his newly hard-earned reputation among the Mongols, Temüjin decided to claim his bride. Without Temüjin's enhanced

standing, it is unlikely that the chief of the Onggirats would have allowed his daughter to marry someone possessing merely one tent and nine
horses. The sixteen-year-old Temüjin traveled to the Onggirat's camp and
married Börte, the second powerful woman in his life. For a dowry, the
bride's father gave Temüjin a very valuable sable cloak.

It is clear that the decision to marry was only the beginning of Temüjin's
plan to gain control of his future, a future in which he was determined to
become one of the leaders—if not *the* leader—of the Mongol tribes. Not
long after his marriage, Temüjin paid a visit to his father's old anda, Toghril,
the chieftain of the large and powerful Kereit Mongol tribe. By reminding
Toghril of his close ties to Temüjin's father and giving him the sable coat as
a gift, Temüjin convinced the Kereit leader to take him on as a vassal in an
alliance, and even as an adopted son. As part of the alliance, Toghril confirmed Temüjin as chief of the whole Borjigin clan. One cannot exaggerate
the importance of this alliance to Temüjin's future. By coming under the
protection of a powerful steppe leader, Temüjin was given time to focus on
building up his own position without having to worry too much about
assaults from minor tribes and clans. For Toghril's part, he had brought
under his wing an up-and-coming young Mongol leader, further strengthening his own position as a leader on the steppes.

Temüjin did not have long to savor his new position among the
Mongols, since less than a year later, in summer 1184, his still-small band
was attacked by a force of three hundred Merkits. According to the records
of the time, the Merkits had waited nearly twenty years to exact their
revenge on Yesügei for taking the wife of their chief. Before the Merkit
gang could reach the camp, Temüjin and most of the others had mounted
their horses and galloped off. Left behind were Börte and Yesügei's second
wife. The Merkits, intent on catching and killing Temüjin, but disappointed that he and the others had escaped, were delighted when they
captured the two women: "We've got our revenge. We've taken their wives
from them!"[5]

Whatever his reasons for not taking his wife with him as he escaped,
Temüjin risked losing a serious amount of prestige if he did nothing about
her capture. Immediately he called upon his sovereign, Toghril, for assistance. Toghril granted his request for help and personally lead a force of
about twenty thousand Kereits. Temüjin also sent for assistance from his

anda, Jamuga. This request was also swiftly granted, and Jamuga sent a messenger to relay to Temüjin these words: "I have learned that the bed of my anda Temüjin has been made empty, and there is sorrow in my heart. . . . We will have vengeance . . . we will restore [Börte] to him."[6] Committing to such a dangerous enterprise as warring with the Merkits was not something Jamuga would have entertained lightly. And Jamuga is not represented as an impetuous individual in the historical records. Clearly he saw an alliance with Toghril to attack and weaken the Merkits as something to be desired, something that would bring more benefit to him and his tribe than a reputation for loyalty to an anda. Within a few days a combined force of tens of thousands rode off to the Merkit encampment.

Interestingly, although Temüjin came with less than a dozen of his own men while Toghril and Jamuga each brought thousands, he was considered an equal in the planning of the strategy for the coming assault. After a grueling forced ride through the forestlands of the upper Onon and across marshes and lesser rivers, the allied force launched a surprise assault on the Merkit camp, which was arrayed along the Selenga River. The attack was at night and in force. Jamuga laid out the plan of attack: his forces were to attack in tight formation with the shock of the initial assault leaving the mass of the Merkits too stunned to resist. The guards heard the rumbling of the galloping horses and were able to send up a shout to awaken the tribe, but there was no time to organize resistance.

Success came swiftly, but we do not know from the record exactly what role Temüjin played in the attack. That he was considered an equal of Toghril and Jamuga, though he personally commanded only a handful of men, demonstrates the confidence and reputation he had already gained. We do know that Temüjin, once reunited with his wife, displayed his tender side when he closely embraced her. The other captive, Yesügei's second wife, had been terribly abused, and in their revenge the combined forces slaughtered many of the Merkit prisoners and their wives and children.

Temüjin was surprised to find Börte pregnant. Most likely this was not Temüjin's biological child but of one of the Merkits', but when Börte gave birth he accepted the son, Jöchi ("guest"), as his own. Possibly this was Temüjin's way of showing regret for originally abandoning Börte when the Merkits had attacked his camp. In most ways Jöchi was indeed treated as Temüjin's own son, but his suspect origins dogged Temüjin through-out his life.

The attack on the Merkits to recover Börte was by far the largest, most complex battle in Temüjin's young life. There were murmurs among his allies about his breaking off in the middle of the fighting to find his wife, but otherwise he had acquitted himself very well and had enhanced his reputation and prestige. Temüjin now worked toward his goal for the next stage of his life—to strengthen his position as Toghril's designated successor.

Unification of Mongolia

T HE BATTLE TO RESCUE Börte was more than simply a fight among tribes. While our knowledge of specific details is lacking, we do know that many were impressed by Temüjin's demonstration of his fighting skills and leadership abilities. And Temüjin's treatment of his wife and new child also illustrate his reverence for loyalty, regardless of his son's dubious origins. Temüjin's (and the world's, for that matter) life took a turn at this point. While few would have predicted it at the time, Temüjin was now on a path that eventually led to his leadership of the steppe lands. Whatever his specific actions prior to and during the battle against the Merkits, Temüjin's newly earned respect also led to newfound suspicion and jealousy among his allies.

With his legitimacy as a possible heir to Toghril and recent success in battle, Temüjin began to amass a large number of recruits for his tribe. But this new power and influence also brought with it new problems, especially with his ally and anda, Jamuga. After the war with the Merkits, the two allies rode together and their tribes pastured their animals together. They even renewed their vows of blood brotherhood. But, at some point in 1185—and for unclear reasons—the two had a falling out, and Temüjin took his followers and their flocks and left the encampment.

The break between the men became clear during the summer of 1185 as the tribes traveled looking for camping sites. Jamuga suggested that he lead the horses to one spot and Temüjin lead the sheep and goat herders to camp in a different spot. Confused over the meaning of this suggestion, Temüjin prepared to ask his mother for help. However, before he could get her advice, Börte spoke up: "They say anda Jamuga's a fickle man. I think the time's come when he's finally grown tired of us. These words are meant to cover some kind of plot. When he stops, let's not pitch our camp. Let's tell our people to keep right on moving, and if we travel all night, by daybreak our camps will be well separated."[1] That night Temüjin and his followers quietly left the camp and traveled many miles before stopping. Obviously, he and his band feared that Jamuga would come after them. In addition to Temüjin's own clan members, several other clans, families, and individuals broke with Jamuga and joined Temüjin, most important Subodei, who would later become one of the most successful of Genghis Khan's generals. The defections from his tribe enraged Jamuga, but, at least for a while, he did not pursue Temüjin and his followers.

The split has never been convincingly explained, but most scholars agree that Jamuga was probably attempting to assert himself as the superior leader in the relationship and Temüjin, prodded by his wife and mother, would not accept this subordinate status.[2] In fact, the incident has been used to portray Temüjin as overly influenced by women. The break led to nearly twenty years of warfare between the two former friends and forced nearly all in Mongolia to choose sides in the growing civil war for dominance. Over the years Temüjin was successful in pulling families, clans, tribes, and important individuals away from their alliance with Jamuga.

The defectors did not shift their alliance because of any special sense of kinship or family ties with Temüjin. As we have seen already, alliances on the steppes were almost always fragile, as leaders sought the most benefit for themselves and their clans and subclans as well as protection from other Mongol alliances. Over the years Temüjin demonstrated military and political competence, and he also acquired a reputation as a fair judge who did not play favorites. Temüjin's reputation did not spread only by word of mouth. He was also quite adept at promoting himself through the use of the cultural tools available. His image was greatly enhanced through the use of shamans—especially his personal friend Kokochu—who spread tales of omens favorable to Temüjin. The tribes often conducted successful raids, and Temüjin changed the manner in which the spoils of the raids were divided. Traditionally, the various tribe and clan leaders divided what they had acquired. Temüjin required that all booty be placed in a common pile, and he then divided it among the leaders, who in turn rewarded their followers. In this way, Temüjin not only created a more efficient means of dividing the spoils of war, but he also emphasized his own supreme leadership. All rewards were granted by Temüjin, thus reinforcing his role as leader and his direct connection with the common Mongol soldier.

In 1189, less than two years after initiating the build up of his new tribe, both in numbers and in wealth, Temüjin took a very bold and decisive step. He gathered the leaders of the various families, clans, and tribes under his leadership and made a claim for the title of Khan. Now, the title "Khan" (often translated as "leader" or "chief" or even "king," depending on the context) was not an unusual one on the steppes and was often awarded to leaders of larger tribes, such as the Naiman and Kereits. However, Temüjin's followers were a diverse lot and not quite large enough to merit a Khan as leader. But the groundwork that Temüjin had laid, both directly and through the shamans, persuaded the leaders to accept this enhanced status for their supreme leader. His success in battle and in leadership had convinced them that they were allied with a winner. And the timely arrival of an omen that foretold Temüjin would be ruler of the world did not hurt his cause either.[3] At a *Kuriltay* (assembly of elders and other tribal leaders) that year, Temüjin was proclaimed "Khan," and from this point forward he became known as "Genghis Khan," or, essentially, ruler of the world. However, as was understood at the time, the title was merely a boast until he had succeeded in gaining more complete control of the Mongolian tribes.

After accepting the title and new name, Temüjin (as he was still referred to until 1206) took several steps to ensure his position and prevent opposition from Toghril, his nominal overlord. He immediately sent messengers to Toghril to inform him of his new title and to ask for his blessing. Temüjin's constant solicitation of—and constant stream of gifts to—Toghril paid off, and the old Khan not only gave his blessing but also offered his assistance to Temüjin. Toghril also had fairly good relations with Jamuga at this time, and he probably believed these two leaders balanced out each other and thus formed a lesser threat to his own position. Temüjin had also demonstrated his loyalty to Toghril, and his new title could be seen as further cementing the alliance. Temüjin also reorganized his tribe, replacing clan, subclan, and even family units with new ones of his creation. Each answered to him and were thus dependent on him. He also created his own special bodyguard, later to be called the *keshig*.

At this time Jamuga was busy preparing for a clash with his former *anda*. In summer 1187 he gathered nearly thirty thousand warriors and declared war on Temüjin and his band. Jamuga used a minor incident to justify the attack: one of Temüjin's followers stole a horse and subsequently killed one of Jamuga's relatives. He called for revenge for this slight to his family, and in the ensuing battle Temüjin's forces were completely routed. Temüjin was forced to flee, but he vowed to some day force Jamuga to pay for causing this shame. The easy victory emboldened Jamuga, and he brutalized the captives taken in this war. His followers beheaded two of Temüjin's lieutenants and then tied their heads to the tail of Jamuga's horse. Seventy other captives were executed by being placed alive in cauldrons of boiling water. This seemed cruel even to Mongols, and quite a few of Jamuga's allies soon broke with him and presented themselves to Temüjin.

Although devastating, the defeat was not final, and Temüjin was able to recover and continue his challenge for dominance of the steppe. His reputation for fairness and reward based on merit was attractive to many, especially in comparison to Jamuga's reliance on traditional hierarchy and reward based on status. At this point in the records, though, is a mysterious, almost ten-year gap in the life of Temüjin. Exactly how he recovered from Jamuga's attack and the specifics of his acquisition of more followers and territory from about 1187 to 1196 are not listed in any of the sources. One Chinese source states that Temüjin was a "slave" of the Jin during this period, which may indicate that he had accepted a subordinate status to the Jin rulers in Zhongdu and served as their agent to keep order on the steppe. It is known that by the end of this period Temüjin was one of the major players in Mongolia.

The year 1196 saw Temüjin and his Mongols replace the Tatars as the main steppe allies of Jin China. The Chinese had always worried about a unified Mongolia and did whatever they could to keep the tribes divided

and at war with each other. At times China would favor one tribe, reward-
ing it with wealth and honors in exchange for its service as a "regulator" of
the other tribes. The Jurchen Jin dynasty ruled northern China in the
twelfth century and since the 1160s had utilized the Tatars in this role. But
by the 1190s the Jin worried that the Tatars were becoming too powerful
and independent, at times even launching raids into China, and so they
dropped their support and looked for another regulator. Temüjin saw an
opportunity and took it. In addition to the power, wealth, and prestige
that came with an alliance with China, Temüjin was also interested in
revenge, as it was a Tatar band that had poisoned his father.

This was also a year in which Temüjin came to the aid of Toghril after
his overlord had been overthrown by his brother. Toghril had managed to
escape with a few followers and sought refuge in Kara-Khitai. He remained
there for about a year, but, under circumstances that are not quite clear, he
was forced to return to Mongolia. The former leader of nearly a third of
Mongolia's land and people now found it necessary to request help from
his nominal subordinate, for without support he would find it difficult to
survive. Temüjin not only allowed Toghril to join him but also pledged to
help restore him to leadership of the Kereits.

First, they needed to deal with the Tatars. The Tatars had already
rebelled against the Jin in 1195, and there were running battles between
the two forces. In 1196 the Tatars were in retreat, but the Jin wanted a
clear-cut victory. The records are vague regarding whether the Jin commander sent an emissary to Temüjin or the first step of requesting an
alliance came from Temüjin. But an alliance of some sort was worked out
with Toghril (as the nominal superior) and Temüjin, and they agreed to a
general strategy for dealing with the Tatars.

The Tatars were camped along the Ulja River, and advance forces of the
Jin occupied the nearby hills to the south. The Jin cavalry forces moved
from the south and chased the Tatars directly into the waiting forces of
Temüjin and Toghril. The Tatar leader and his bodyguard attempted to
escape but were chased down by Temüjin and killed. Although many
other Tatars did escape and some of the clans were camped elsewhere at the
time of the battle and did not participate in the fighting, the Tatars' power
was broken and the power of the Kereit-Mongol alliance was greatly enhanced. As part of the reward for assisting in the defeat of the Tatars, in

1197 the Jin awarded Toghril the title of "Wang" (or "King") of the Kereits. From this time onward he is usually referred to as "Wang-khan." Soon after, Temüjin led his forces to defeat the new Kereit leader and restore Wang-khan to rule.

Steppe politics were extremely complicated, with shifting alliances, marriage and kin relations, defections, assassinations, and rebellions, but both Temüjin and Wang-khan were experienced players in the game. In restoring Wang-khan to power, Temüjin acted as loyal vassal. He greatly admired loyalty in character, but he had other motives for his support as well. In return for restoring him to power, Wang-khan made Temüjin heir to the Kereit throne. Unlike in the past, when Temüjin was dependent on Wang-khan's support, now the roles were reversed, and Wang-khan was not pleased with the situation. Soon after regaining power, he led a raid on a major Merkit encampment. Victory was total and the spoils were plentiful. However, in a calculated insult, Wang-khan did not invite Temüjin to join in the attack, and Temüjin did not receive any of the spoils. Wang-khan also began to show more favor to his son, Senggüm, a clear indication of his preference for successor.

In 1198 Wang-khan invited Temüjin to join him in attacking on the Kereits' perennial enemies, the Naiman. At this point the Naiman were divided, with each of the two groups ruled by a son of the previous ruler. Half kept their camps in the Altai Mountain region, the other half on the steppes. The Kereit-Mongol alliance attacked the Altai Naiman first. After several successful skirmishes against small bands and camps, the alliance came upon the main Naiman force, which had at its side Jamuga and his followers. Both sides hunkered down for the evening in preparation for a major battle the next day. During the night Wang-khan took his men and slipped away, leaving Temüjin and his Mongols to face the Naiman alone. It seems apparent that Wang-khan expected Temüjin to be killed or captured in battle, or at least seriously wounded. But Wang-khan's plan backfired when the Naiman, seeing their enemy divided, decided to go after what they believed to be the more powerful force—that of Wang-khan's. The Kereit leader and his battlefield commander, his son Senggüm, were in dire straights and sent messengers to Temüjin urgently requesting aid. Temüjin's timely arrival prevented a defeat from turning into a disaster. In return, Wang-khan publicly named Temüjin heir to the Kereit throne.

While dramatic, this honor was merely one more step on Temüjin's path to becoming supreme ruler of Mongolia, for there were still many tribes and clans independent of him or openly hostile, including the dangerous tribe led by Jamuga.

In 1200 Jamuga called a Kuriltay of several steppe tribes and Mongol clans who were not allied with Temüjin, including the remaining Merkits, Taichiuts, and Tatars. At this Kuriltay, Jamuga was proclaimed "Gur-khan," or ruler of all the Mongol tribes, a title previously held by Wang-khan's father. Jamuga's alliance was larger than that of Wang-khan and Temüjin's, but it was not as well controlled, nor was it as reliable.

In the late fall of that year the two sides clashed in the Argun Valley. This might have been the decisive battle, but a fierce snowstorm broke out, and Jamuga was forced to withdraw with most of his forces. Temüjin chased after one faction of the enemy, the Taichiut clan, along the Onon River, the region of his birth. The Taichiuts were the people who had captured Temüjin when he was fifteen, enslaving him and putting him in a cangue. In fierce fighting Temüjin was wounded by an arrow to the neck. His loyal subordinate, Jelme, cared for his wounds and sucked out the blood from the wound in order not to worry the troops nor encourage the enemy. The next day, Temüjin led his troops in a rout of the enemy. In revenge for the humiliation the Taichiut inflicted on him as a prisoner many years ago, he ordered the slaughter of all the male Taichiut inhabitants. The women and children were distributed among his men.

During the battle, Temüjin's horse was felled with an arrow. When the prisoners were gathered, he demanded to know who had shot his horse. A young man, a low-ranking soldier, stepped forward and boldly asserted that he had accomplished the deed. Temüjin was greatly impressed at the man's courage and willingness to take responsibility for his actions. The solider was not only spared but also made an officer in Temüjin's army and given the name "Jebe," or "Arrow." Temüjin once again proved himself a master in judging character: Jebe went on to become one of Genghis Khan's greatest generals.[4]

With his following growing larger, Temüjin decided to finish off the Tatars once and for all. Despite their defeat by the Kereit-Mongol alliance in 1196, the Tatars were still a power to be reckoned with, mainly because of their large numbers. In attacking the Tatars, it is also likely that Temüjin was preparing for a confrontation with his nominal superior, Wang-khan. The Tatar lands were to the east of Temüjin and Wang-khan's lands were to his west. Defeating the Tatars would prevent a possible two-front war.

The Tatars greatly outnumbered Temüjin's forces, and so in preparation he had his men engage in constant large- and small-unit drill and practice. It was during this intensive training that Temüjin issued his famous order regarding plunder. Distribution of plunder was centralized in his hands and was to take place after a battle had been settled. Any individual who took what had not yet been apportioned would face severe punishment. This new rule was so unlike any tradition among the nomadic peoples of the steppes that it threatened to disrupt and even dissolve his army. However, since Temüjin's army was already centralized to a great degree, in loyalty and leadership at least, the edict did not provoke dissent. Temüjin's fierce reputation served to quiet some who found his order troubling.

When battle came in 1202, a greatly outnumbered Mongol force surprised the Tatars, and strict Mongol military discipline led to swift victory. As with the battle against the Taichiuts, Temüjin ordered the extermination of the Tatar tribe males, finally satisfied that he had now gained revenge for the death of his father. The few Tatar males who did survive were distributed throughout the Mongol army as soldiers.

While Temüjin was seemingly at the height of his power and influence, the old Kereit leader was listening to his son and the ever-ambitious and resourceful Jamuga. They pointed to Temüjin's rising prestige as a direct threat to the Kereit position. In 1202 they persuaded Wang-khan to denounce Temüjin and place Senggüm as his heir. Kereit forces were put under the command of Jamuga, who had recovered some of the alliances he had previously lost. In summer 1203, the Kereit attacked and defeated Temüjin and his followers. Much looting and slaughter followed the defeat, but Temüjin and a handful of his closest followers escaped. After this treatment at the hands of his former blood brother and his former mentor, it is no wonder that Temüjin believed blood ties and sworn oaths were next to useless. But his charisma and reputation as a great leader allowed him to quickly recover most of his allies. He even forged new alliances with the Uighur, Khitan, and Tangut tribes. Several wealthy Muslim merchants also approached him to offer their assistance. It is not always clear from the sources what Temüjin did to gain all of these alliances, but those who joined with him believed that the future of the region lay with him and not Jamuga, and certainly not the aging Wang-khan.

Temüjin moved very quickly, and within three months of his defeat he had reconstructed much of his former force. While he sneered at the value of oaths and kinship on the steppes, Temüjin at the same time had become very skilled in using these concepts to draw out defectors from his enemies. He understood that many of Wang-khan's alliances were not secure and he convinced several tribes to join his Mongol force.

Wang-khan, Jamuga, and their followers spent these months celebrating what they believed had been a decisive victory. They were disabused of this notion in late fall 1203 when Temüjin attacked the Kereit-Jamuga alliance in a battle that lasted three days. With Mukali, one of Temüjin's great commanders who would later distinguish himself in China, in the lead, a force of several thousand marched very quickly at night to where Wang-khan was camped, a defile near the confluence of the Onon and Tula rivers. They struck at daybreak, and, although the Kereits fought hard, the Mongols kept their discipline and would not be denied a decisive victory. Temüjin absorbed the large number of surrendered and captured Kereits into his own tribe. They were not slaughtered or treated as slaves but as new members of the Mongol tribe. Wang-khan escaped and attempted to seek refuge with the Naiman, his old enemies. They did not see any advantage to having him around, so they killed him. The Naiman did, however, give refuge to Jamuga and his remaining followers, setting up an inevitable clash with Temüjin and his Mongols.

Barely a year later, in spring 1204, Temüjin led his army against the Naiman, the only major force left that could prevent Temüjin from unifying Mongolia. The Naiman greatly outnumbered the Mongols, but Temujin used a number of ruses (such as lighting hundreds of extra campfires each night) to convince the Naiman that he commanded a much larger force. Several small skirmishes took place along the western foothills of the Hangay Mountains, and Temüjin used his newly organized army to systematically destroy the Naiman force. The Naiman ruler and his generals tried to lead the Mongols into a prepared trap by using an old nomadic standby, the feigned retreat. Expecting to encounter a disorganized opponent, the Naiman instead attacked a well-disciplined and well-prepared Mongol force. The defeat of the Naiman was complete, and, like the Kereits, their clan members were distributed among Temüjin's various Mongol units.

Jamuga managed to escape and wander the forestlands for another year before his remaining followers delivered him to the Mongols. For their disloyalty to their leader, these men were beheaded. Temüjin then had Jamuga crushed to death, but did not seem to enjoy the destruction of his former anda.[5]

Now master of Mongolia, Temüjin prepared for the ceremony at which he would formally accept the ruling title of Genghis Khan, which had been conferred on him back in 1189. As part of his preparation Temüjin took several steps to ensure he had true control over Mongolia. In one important move, he sent the young Mongol commander Subodei into the northern reaches of Mongolia to subdue the remaining forest tribes. Subodei met with success on this campaign, the start of his role as the greatest of Genghis Khan's commanders.

In addition to subduing the northern forest peoples, Temüjin also arranged for his shamans to produce propaganda to convince the people of his divine approval. Kokochu—who was not only his personal shaman but also the most respected shaman in the region—claimed Tengri told him Temüjin was his representative on earth.

The Kuriltay of 1206 saw Temüjin take the title of Genghis Khan, offered this time by the united tribes of Mongolia and not just a faction of those tribes. The Kuriltay also proclaimed him ruler of all those "who live in felt tents," referring not only to the Mongols, but also to all nomadic peoples of Mongolia. From this time on, he declared that all such people were to be known as "Mongols," though the actual Mongols were only one among many tribal peoples on the steppe.

Genghis Khan had secured his power "based on his personal prowess in war, his hereditary descent from the ancient khans of Mongolia, and an invincible success which betokened to the people the benign approval of heaven."[6] There was no doubt who was the lord of the territories of the "people who live in felt tents," but to keep this power Genghis Khan needed more than past victories and his reputation. As he had learned through much difficulty, the loyalty of his people had to be constantly nurtured or he would lose it. Thus, he was aware that he needed new victories and the spoils those victories brought in order to keep his people united and under his rule. In achieving these aims, Genghis Khan would prove to be the most successful conqueror in history.

Mongol Military System

A[FTER GENGHIS KHAN] gained control over Mongolia, the social structure remained mostly unchanged from traditional structures. Tribes and clans operated as they had for centuries. At least, those that had not been exterminated during the wars of unification were unaltered. And so, it is not quite right to call Genghis Khan a revolutionary in a social or even political sense. But the structure of the Mongol military that the Great Khan organized can be called revolutionary. So it should be no surprise that this restructuring of the military was what led to dramatic changes in Mongol society.

Most of the Mongol military system was actually fashioned by Genghis Khan in the years just prior to the Kuriltay of 1206, a result of the hard lessons he had learned during years of struggle and warfare. The most important lesson he had learned was he could not rely on family or even traditional chiefs when choosing subordinate commanders. He resolved to look for proven ability and unswerving loyalty in his commanders. While Genghis Khan often appointed his sons commanders of expeditions, they always had with them a competent, experienced subordinate who usually acted as the real commander. Both the sons of the Khan and the men under them understood this arrangement.

Genghis Khan's Mongols employed the decimal system of organiza-tion—the division of the military forces into units of ten. This approach was not unique to the Mongols, but their implementation of the method was unique. Similarly, most of the tactics and styles of fighting used by the Mongols were also common for the Inner Asian steppe region. What was atypical was the unity and discipline of the Mongols under Genghis Khan's leadership and instruction. In effect, he took what was already a formidable group of warriors and turned them into a massively powerful military force.

Prior to unification, Genghis Khan had already organized the Mongol warriors into commands of one thousand men, each unit called a *minghan*. While most of the commanders of these minghan were traditional clan or tribal leaders, by 1206 all had been appointed or confirmed by the Great Khan. The whole army was by this time further divided into a decimal system: groups of ten, then one hundred, then one thousand (still called minghan). Again, this was not particularly unique on the steppes. Yet, Genghis Khan added another level of organization, with ten units of minghan forming a group of ten thousand, called a *tümen*. This clearly indicates that he was planning for large-scale campaigns that would require these larger military units.

Commanders at each level were responsible to not only the next higher commander but directly to Genghis Khan himself. During or soon after the Kuriltay, Genghis Khan completed the personal appointment of all commanders of tümens and minghans. Quite a large number of lower-level commanders were also personally appointed by the Khan, something unprecedented on the steppes.

As part of a strategy to break tribal unities and forge new loyalty toward him, Genghis Khan placed individuals from different tribes and clans in units. For example, he divided surviving Tatars and Kereits among many units in the army. Genghis had learned through bitter experience not to trust traditional elites on the steppes, and by splitting up tribes and clans, he made it much harder for commanders to threaten his position. Unit cohesion and discipline was maintained even at the lowest level—units of ten. Collective punishment was meted on the whole unit if even one of their number violated the rules.[1] In the process of reorganization Genghis Khan created not just a new "tribe," but a much more united and effective fighting force.

Early in the process of creating this new fighting force, Genghis Khan laid down numerous military regulations. Such rules covered the order of march into battle, organization of night camps, maintenance of weaponry, and relations among the Mongol tribesmen. Punishments were very harsh. One rule even stated that an incompetent leader was to be executed.[2] While scholars debate the degree to which these rules were actually enforced, it is very hard to imagine that Genghis Khan would issue rules that were not intended to be implemented and obeyed.

The most innovative and significant of the institutions that Genghis Khan established at the Kuriltay of 1206 was the keshig. The keshig began as Genghis Khan's elite personal bodyguard, possibly modeled after the bodyguard units of the Khitans, but by 1206 the keshig numbered exactly ten thousand and included a hand-picked group of one thousand men called *baturs* ("braves"). Nothing like it had ever existed before among the steppe nomads. Membership of the keshig came from the army ranks, but the officers of the guard all came from traditional Mongol-leading families and, especially, from the families of the Khan's minghan and tümen commanders. Most keshig officers were younger brothers or sons of these leading commanders, serving then not only as bodyguards for Genghis Khan but also as hostages for the good behavior of their relatives. Genghis Khan also hoped that these younger brothers and sons would eventually develop a personal tie of loyalty to him.

The keshig rarely went into battle except with Genghis Khan himself, and they served as a sort of general staff as well as a training ground for future leaders. In addition, the Great Khan used the keshig to supply leadership replacements. Most of the later Mongol commanders began as keshig officers, and, once again, we see Genghis Khan relying not on his family (none of whom were members of the keshig) but on others of proven loyalty and competence. The keshig, its organization, and the uses to which it was put were all very unusual in Mongolia, but Genghis Khan and his successors benefited greatly from this innovation.

Even prior to Genghis Khan's unification of the tribes, every able-bodied adult Mongol male was considered liable for military duties, making Mongolia truly a nation in arms. The Mongol soldier was by any measure an incredible fighting man. The Mongols expected boys to begin learning to ride their ponies from the age of three, and at age five the young

Mongol who had successfully learned to ride was given his first bow and arrows and expected to spend a good deal of his time hunting on horseback. These hunts often lasted for days without stopping, and the tribe expected the fit Mongol to sleep in the saddle rather than delay the whole group. By age sixteen, after years of hardship and training, a Mongol boy was finally deemed ready to be considered a full-fledged Mongol warrior.

The main weapon of the Mongol was the composite bow, with a draw of nearly 165 pounds, and an accuracy that often reached 200–300 yards. When leaving for battle the Mongol typically carried two bows and three quivers with about thirty each of the two main types of arrows, one for short distance and the other for long distance. He might also carry in his quiver armor-piercing arrows and whistling arrows. Some Mongols trained on longbows, useful for firing long distances, and most carried some sort of sword or, at times, a lance with a hook on the end. During the campaigns in northern China, the Mongols began to wear a silk shirt underneath their armor. This was not evidence that the Mongols had become soft with the luxuries of China but served a very useful military role. In addition to affording more freedom of movement for the arms and torso, the silk would wrap around an enemy arrow that might pierce the Mongol's armor. The arrow could be carefully removed without causing additional damage to the body.

Training for battle also took the form of hunts, and after Genghis Khan had unified the tribes, he led them on several very large-scale hunts. In these hunts, a large area would be cordoned off and beaters would chase the animals toward the ring of Mongols. After all the animals had been killed, the commanders would critique the hunt as if it had been a major military campaign.

When going into battle the Mongol warrior usually took along spare horses, rarely fewer than three. The Mongols trained these horses to respond to voice commands and to maintain their speed and balance as a Mongol shot arrows both in front and toward the rear of the horse. Each Mongol also carried a short sword as well as sometimes a short lance with an attached hook, which the Mongol used to pull opponents out of the saddle. Other equipment taken along included a hatchet, a file for sharpening arrow heads, a rope for pulling wagons, an iron cooking pot, leather bottles, and a leather bag that contained jerky, needles and thread, a fur helmet, a small tent, and other items that might be needed while traveling to the field of battle. This leather bag was also waterproof in order to protect the bag's contents when crossing bodies of water. For armor, the Mongol was equipped with a steel helmet with a leather neckpiece and layered hides that were lacquered to protect them from humidity, or overlapping scales of iron laced together. The hide armor was usually made of six layers sown tightly together, softened by boiling, and molded to fit the body. Mongol warriors had their choice of various types of shields though they usually carried only a small one when on the attack, and they used this primarily to ward off enemy arrows.

In the first invasions, in addition to the kit and several ponies that each Mongol brought along with him, the army lived off the land, devouring the countryside to supply its needs. In later campaigns, the Mongol army needed to employ more sophisticated logistics. Their entourage at times included tens of thousands of non-Mongol auxiliaries, siege engines, and long baggage trains. The lands where these campaigns took place could not always be pillaged for supplies. Therefore, the Mongols established mechanisms for supplying these armies through sometimes extremely brutal plundering of the sedentary populations under their control.

Once the Mongol army conquered a land or its people had accepted Mongol tributary status, the army required the conquered tribal members to provide the foodstuffs, weapons, clothing, carts, draftsmen, workers, and other items deemed necessary. Genghis Khan established a policy very early in his reign in which, upon taking control of a region, the officials of the land were ordered to conduct a thorough record of the population and resources. Officials working directly for the Mongols supervised the reporting. Eventually, it became common for these officials to hail from distant lands in order to prevent collusion with the locals. For example, Mongol officials in China were usually of Persian, Arab, Central Asian, or even European descent, and large numbers of Chinese and Koreans were brought to Persia to administer that land. At first, the Mongols simply took these audit officials from already conquered localities; later, skilled individuals would seek out Mongol officials and offer their services.

The Mongol achievement in logistic tasks cannot be overstated. By the time of Genghis Khan's death, the Mongols had imposed a uniform system of taxation and tribute in several regions with widely varying traditions and administrative systems. While Genghis Khan administered this system from his moveable campaign headquarters, his successors established a capital at Karakorum, in the middle of the steppe lands. The whole system utilized the services of vast numbers of officials with nothing in common other than their service to the Mongol empire.

Most of Mongol strategy and field tactics under Genghis Khan conformed to traditional steppe warfare, especially the use of feigned retreats and ambushes. One very useful and important army innovation was Genghis Khan's insistence that detailed intelligence be acquired and meticulous planning completed prior to launching a major attack on a region. Before engaging an enemy, Mongol commanders were required to become familiar with a region by talking with people familiar with the target territory, including its inhabitants. Mongol military planners consulted Khwarazmian merchants about their homelands and the Chinese about Jin China. Genghis Khan liked to know as much as possible about a target before launching an expedition; he wanted to better understand what he was up against.

Another important innovation was the extensive use of scouts, who were sent out ahead of the main invasion force to note roads, bridges, mountain passes, terrain features, people, enemy units, and just about anything that might be of use to the attacking force behind them. While the use of such scouts was quite common in much of Asia, including the steppe lands, Genghis Khan utilized them far more systematically, as regular, trained units, and they at times played a very important role in the direction or even strategy of a particular campaign. These scouts were also useful in spreading "propaganda" about the Mongols, making them appear far more terrible than they actually were. In the market areas of towns and cities, the scouts would spread stories about the vast size of the Mongol armies, describe in (often made-up) detail the horrors experienced by those captured by the Mongols, and disseminate misdirection about the locations and line of march of Mongol armies.

Genghis Khan trained his subordinates to rely on all the traditional battle tactics but also to be open to impromptu innovation. At times, he would have his units tie branches to their horses' tails so when they rode, the dust that was kicked up would make it look like there were far more men than they really had. Or, the army would gather thousands of local people to march in front of the army, making it appear that these thousands were part of the Mongol army, and they would be the first to be hit when attacked. Another related tactic was to take advantage of the enemies of their targets, such as when the Mongols formed an alliance with the Southern Song Chinese to attack Jin China. Mongol military flexibility was one of their greatest weapons, and Genghis Khan demanded that his men be ready to adopt the tactics of their enemies if that would help them. This turned out to be especially useful thinking when the Mongols were faced with fortified cities.

In the earliest campaigns against Xi Xia and Jin China, Genghis Khan faced the greatest impediment to Mongol military success, fortified cities. Some of the fortifications around Chinese cities, for example, were tremendously large and complex and impossible for a cavalry force to take. Rather than try to quickly retrain the Mongols in siege warfare, Genghis Khan employed Chinese who were experienced in the art of siege craft. He set thousands of Chinese to work to build the siege engines and to travel with the Mongol army to operate them. By the time he led his armies against the Khwarazm Empire and Persia, several units of Chinese and their siege engines accompanied the army. The Chinese siege units also brought with them gunpowder weapons, such as exploding bombs and flaming explosives.

The papal envoy Carpini in 1245 described Mongol siege tactics:

> If a place is well fortified they surround it and securely hedge it in so that no one can get in or out, and they fight fiercely with machines and arrows and do not stop the attack by day or night, so that those in the fort can not rest. . . . If they cannot take the place that way, they throw Greek Fire. In fact, they sometimes take the grease of the men they kill and throw it liquefied onto the houses, and wherever this grease catches fire it burns as though it cannot be extinguished. . . . If the Tartars do not prevail in this way and the city or camp has a river, they block it or they make another riverbed and submerged the fort if they can."[3]

In battle, the Mongols were experts at the feint, or what is often called the "feigned retreat." This involved the Mongol force retreating in the middle of a battle, apparently in disorder. As the enemy, convinced they had won, chased the Mongols, they themselves became disordered. At a signal or a predetermined spot or time, the Mongols would suddenly wheel around, form up, and attack in order. Even a much larger enemy force would be hard-pressed to regain its discipline and, in fact, enemy warriors often fled. Other times a feigned retreat was initiated in order to lead an enemy into a set ambush. Another related tactic was to have the Mongol center retreat, thus weakening the center. After the enemy force pushed forward by attacking the center, they would then find their flanks under fierce assault. Although similar, there is no evidence that the Mongols were aware of Hannibal's strategy in the Battle of Cannae.

The Mongols also perfected the "arrow storm." This was a shock tactic designed to disorient the enemy with volleys of arrows from the light cavalry, weakening it for the charge from the heavy cavalry. The Mongol archers carried this out by riding back and forth in front of the enemy as they loosed their arrows, or, at times, the arrow storm would be directed at a central point or points of the enemy line. In battles in China and Persia, the arrow storm was often enough to cause an enemy cavalry force to flee rapidly to their rear, disrupting their own infantry forces. One should keep in mind that tactics such as these were not new to steppe armies—the Khitans probably best employed the arrow storm strategy prior to the Mongols. Yet, these earlier nomadic armies rarely engaged in more than small-unit training. Genghis Khan's great innovation was to emphasize constant training in these tactics, especially with large-scale units of tens of thousands.

In yet another innovation by Genghis Khan, during battle Mongol chief commanders positioned themselves somewhat to the rear of the Mongol army, allowing them to follow the flow of the battle and to initiate changes as they saw fit. Junior officers equipped with flags, bugles, or, at night, with lamps relayed commands to the front lines.

Finally, terror was a major instrument of the Mongol military's strategic efforts and was designed to demoralize an enemy and weaken his will to resist. In order to achieve this goal, the entire population of a city might be marched out and divided among the Mongol warriors for slaughter or moats filled in with the corpses of people from the surrounding country-side. These and other acts of terror contributed to the Mongols' reputation among Muslims and Christians as soldiers from Hell, come to punish a sinful land.

Genghis Khan also stressed to his subordinate commanders that a defeated enemy must be pursued and completely destroyed to prevent them from being able to regroup. When an enemy fled the field, the Mongols pursued them and slaughtered as many as they could. Sometimes the Mongols would chase defeated enemies over thirty miles, and, in one recorded case, they chased defeated enemies over two hundred miles. Genghis Khan's incursions into Afghanistan and northern India were in large part a result of his chase after the remnants of the Khwarazmian army. Only when the Mongols were too tired or had won only a marginal victory would they pass up the pursuit of their defeated enemies. In other instances, the Mongols' attention was required elsewhere and caused them to wait and finish the job another day, as was the case with the Xi Xia, in which Genghis Khan waited nearly twenty years before returning to finish off this kingdom.

The soldiers of the central armies of Genghis Khan were hardened by their life on the steppes, and by the time they were young adults they were experts in the uses of the standard Mongol weapons and tactics. By 1206 they were also adept at fighting major combat operations through constant drills and training in large units. They were ready to move out of the Mongolian heartland, wreak havoc, and begin to conquer the largest empire in history.

Assault on Xi Xia and Jin China

As important as it was, reorganization of the Mongol military was not the only matter that occupied Genghis Khan in the years after the Kuriltay of 1206. He also instituted a new set of laws and rules to govern the people. Although Genghis Khan was illiterate himself (as were nearly all the Mongols), he had been impressed that the Naiman ruler had an Uighur scribe to keep records of his doings and rulings. The chief Uighur scribe of the Naiman was given the same position with the new Mongol nation, and, at the same time, Genghis Khan commanded that the Uighur script be applied to the Mongol language. He also commanded that his sons should be taught this new script. Unfortunately, only fragments of the laws set down by Genghis Khan have survived to the present day.

Genghis Khan, in planning for his empire, utilized trusted followers and men of merit even while placing his sons in positions of nominal authority above these men. He destroyed the traditional aristocracy and hierarchy that had dominated the steppe lands for centuries. Individuals were moved from tribe to tribe or, more accurately, from military unit to military unit. He forbade such Mongol customs as kidnapping women for wives, feuds among clans, and rustling animals from other Mongol clans and tribes. In addition, he ordered a complete census to be taken of the people in this new nation, and grazing lands were noted and allocated.[1]

Genghis Khan's reorganization of Mongol society and institutionalization of laws ran contrary to the traditions of Central Asia. Indeed, no former leader of a large-scale confederation on the steppes—whether Xiongnu, Uighur, or Turk—had attempted such a bold and ambitious undertaking. This was truly a break with the past, and success meant not only that Genghis Khan's personal power was enhanced but also that the Mongols were much more disciplined and effective than any nomadic society in history.

He never neglected the religious aspects of his control of the steppes, and religion often provided Genghis Khan and his successors with the ideological justification for their conquests. In his rise to power, Genghis Khan had utilized the shamanistic religion of the Mongols. His solicitation of the shamans effectively gained him their support. In particular, the endorsement of Kokochu (also known as "Teb-Tengri") was very useful. Prior to major assaults, Genghis Khan would go into isolation to commune with Tengri. It was usual for Tengri to "authorize" the attacks. Kokochu had a reputation that spread across much of the steppe lands, and he was thought to have a special connection with the gods and spirits, especially with Tengri, the chief god of the Mongols. When Kokochu proclaimed that Tengri had called Genghis Khan his personal representative on earth, many heeded. But, after the Kuriltay of 1206, Kokochu sought to enhance his authority beyond the spiritual and religious realm and into the political.

Kokochu's six brothers supported him and spread tales designed to enhance his reputation at the expense of Genghis Khan's. Although his mother warned him about the threat Kokochu posed, Genghis Khan hesitated to act. The most likely explanation for this hesitation was the measure of respect and awe he held for this holy man. Kokochu warned Genghis Khan that his brother Kasar was plotting against him. In fact, Kokochu's brothers had roughed up Kasar, and only the timely intervention of Hoelun saved him from execution. Hoelun died soon after this incident because of other causes. When Genghis Khan began to move against his other brother, Temüge, on the advice of Kokochu, the Khan's wife, Börte, stepped forward and angrily rebuked him. Using similar arguments to those she had used against Jamuga years earlier, Börte convinced her husband to move against Kokochu. Genghis Khan heeded her advice and told Temüge to do whatever he thought was necessary to handle the shaman. Using a ruse to get Kokochu to agree to a wrestling match against Temüge, Temüge caught Kokochu unaware, and, with three aides, he broke Kokochu's back, killing him.[2]

With Kokochu out of the way, Genghis Khan's power was now complete and he faced no serious threat from any quarter of the steppes. Ironically, the killing of Kokochu served to enhance Genghis Khan's reputation for favor with the gods, and he was even referred to as a shaman himself. In this story, we can also see, once again, support for the argument that Genghis Khan allowed himself to be swayed by the admonitions of his mother and his wife. Some accused him of trembling when subject to their anger. However, in this case we can see that heeding their warnings and advice was greatly to his advantage.

The control Genghis Khan solidified over the Mongols would have been short-lived and nothing more than an interesting footnote to history if the new Mongol nation had remained confined to Mongolia. Genghis Khan understood that in order to maintain his control, especially in the early years immediately following unification in 1206, he needed to provide his followers with rewards. Nomadic armies of the steppe lands since Xiongnu had looked to China for the source of these rewards.

After securing his control over Mongolia and much of Central Asia, Genghis Khan turned his attention to the real prize—China, with its vast amount of loot: silks, jewels, food, and metal goods, among other spoils. At that time, China was not a unified empire. Most of southern China was under the rule of the native Chinese Song dynasty. This dynasty controlled all of China (the dynasty was founded in 960), but had had great difficulty defending itself from Mongolian and Manchurian tribal peoples. Much of the northeast came under the control of the Khitans, who themselves were swallowed up by the Jurchens from Manchuria early in the twelfth century. The Khitans who escaped the dominance of the Jurchens fled westward and founded the small kingdom of Kara-Khitai. The Jurchens moved to consolidate their control over northern China, adopted much of the Chinese style of rule, and founded a dynasty they called "Jin." The Song retained control of southern China and attempted many times to regain control over the north, but the Song-Jin stalemate lasted through the early thirteenth century. In fact, a major struggle with the Song in the early years of the thirteenth century was the only reason the Jin did not take action against Genghis Khan as he consolidated his control over Mongolia. Meanwhile, a Tangut kingdom called Xi Xia took over the area of present-day Gansu and instituted its own Chinese-style administration.

China was certainly the big prize, but in order to secure his flank Genghis Khan needed to at least neutralize Xi Xia. Attacking China, even if only to raid and acquire booty, was a major undertaking. The Chinese vastly outnumbered the Mongols and possessed an enormous array of weapons as well as large fortified cities. By assaulting Xi Xia, Genghis Khan could give his forces experience in fighting large-scale battles against a sedentary people and dealing with their walled cities. Thus, in addition to protecting his flank, attacking Xi Xia provided valuable fighting experience to the newly organized Mongol military force. In light of the Mongol interest in open lines of trade, another goal in assaulting Xi Xia was to secure some of the main transit points along the Silk Road.

Less than a year after the 1206 Kuriltay, Genghis Khan sent raiding parties into Xi Xia. The purpose was to acquire loot, of course, in order to maintain the "loyalty" of the subordinate tribes, but also to gain valuable intelligence about the lay of the land, Tangut defenses, weak points, and possible allies. These raids continued during the summer of 1207 and again in the summer of 1208.

The main invasion into Xi Xia territory took place after careful planning in spring 1209. With Genghis Khan personally leading, the army marched several hundred miles through the Gobi Desert before crossing the border. Xi Xia was primarily an agricultural land with a horse-herding industry as well as several well-fortified cities and fortresses. The Tanguts of Xi Xia had tangled with nomadic peoples before and used their fortified cities as bases from which to launch attacks on the raiders. Genghis Khan intended to take these cities, but he found that his Mongols were not very skilled at this task. After defeating several smaller armies that came to meet them, the Mongols became bogged down in a protracted siege of the city of Volohai. The Mongols suffered tremendous losses in their futile assaults against the walls of the city. Rather than bypass the city—the usual no-madic strategy—Genghis Khan decided to use a ruse. According to the stories of the time, the Khan sent a message to the commander of the Volohai garrison stating that the Mongols would leave if the city turned over ten thousand birds and one thousand cats. The dumbfounded commander agreed, and the people of the city gathered up all the birds and cats they could. Once in their possession, the Mongols tied tufts of cotton to the tails of the birds and cats, set the cotton on fire, and let the animals go. With their tails flaming, the hysterical birds and cats fled back to their nests and lairs in the city causing the city to erupt in flames. The Mongols then walked in and looted what was left.[3]

The taking of Volohai marked the first time the Mongols won control of a major fortified city. The Mongols gained valuable experience in a form of warfare they and their nomadic ancestors had always been bedeviled by. Genghis Khan also reconfirmed the value he attached to innovation and resourcefulness. The taking of Volohai, once again, highlights the radical nature of his military leadership. He was not to be limited by traditional notions and methods of nomadic warfare. Success in taking this city also enhanced his political and military authority, as it added greatly to Genghis Khan's prestige among the Mongol warriors.

After the siege of Volohai, the Xi Xia armies retreated to their remaining forts while the Mongols pillaged the countryside. As the Mongol armies became stretched thin during the summer, Xi Xia armies attacked with some success, but by August several more tümen had arrived and Genghis Khan resumed the offensive. By the end of that month, he arrived at the gates of Ningxia, the capital of Xi Xia, located along the Yellow River.

Ningxia was much larger and even better fortified than Volohai had been, and the Mongols became frustrated. An attack and subsequent feigned retreat tricked the Xi Xia commander into committing his main force in a pursuit, and it was cut down and the commander captured. This, however, was not enough to take the city, and the Mongols could not afford to wait too much longer because of the coming of fall and winter. The Mongols built a dam along the Yellow River, hoping to divert the water into the city. But at this time, the Mongols' engineering skill was poor and the water was diverted to the Mongol encampment rather than the city. Fortunately for Genghis Khan, Xi Xia's king requested negotiations. In the peace agreement, the Tangut ruler provided a great deal of tribute, mainly silk, camels, and woolen goods. He also gave one of his daughters in marriage to Genghis

Khan. In addition, the king made vague promises to provide troops for the Mongols, but Xi Xia, in fact, never sent any help to the Mongols.

Xi Xia was now a tributary of the Mongols and was left under the local authority of the king and his court. However, Genghis Khan had lost some face among his warriors over the failed siege of Ningxia. Believing the Khan to be weakened, a group of Merkits and a Naiman prince launched a rebellion in 1210. This was quickly crushed, but Genghis Khan needed more victories to keep his people unified. With Xi Xia no longer a threat, the way was now open to attacking Jin China from the west as well as from the north.

In preparation for the coming war with Jin China, Genghis Khan convened a Kuriltay. He wanted to gain assurances of support from all subordinate tribes. If any of his officers refused to arrive, he would learn the true depth of his support. In his order to appear for the Kuriltay, Genghis Khan stated: "One who remains in his own locality instead of coming to me to receive my instructions will have the fate of a stone dropped into the water—he will disappear."[4] About the same time, the Qarlaq tribal leaders (the Qarlaqs were a tribal nomadic people who lived in the regions to the north, near Lake Balkhash) approached Genghis Khan and asked to submit to his overlordship. More important to Genghis Khan than the additional warriors, now with the Qarlaqs supporting him, his northern flank was secure. Genghis Khan then went to the sacred Mongolian mountain Burkan-Kaldun along the Kerulen River to commune with the gods. With his belt slung over his shoulder in the traditional pose of supplication, Genghis Khan asked the gods for support. For three days on the mountain he fasted, and, when he returned to his encampment, he claimed divine sanction for the coming campaign.

Before launching their attacks, the Mongols were already well informed about their enemy in northern China. The Jin rulers could field an army that totaled roughly 500,000 infantry and at least 120,000 cavalry. The most effective military forces of the Jin were the cavalry units, which came predominantly from the Jurchen tribes that had conquered the land in the previous century. The Jin army also included large numbers of Khitans and Ongguts, who functioned more like mercenary forces. The Khitan troops helped maintain order in their (and the Jurchens') Manchurian homeland, while the Ongguts were a Mongolian tribe that was hired to maintain order along part of the northern border. The infantry was composed over-whelmingly of Chinese. Northern China had a population of about 15–30 million, and many lived in walled and fortified cities. In addition, the Great Wall also protected the northern approaches.[5]

Genghis Khan was acutely aware that the Jin dynasty was not very stable and its control of northern China not very secure. The overwhelming majority of the population was Chinese and not likely to go out of its way to protect the "barbarian" Jurchens from attacks by the "barbarian" Mongols. Rebellions large and small broke out frequently and often kept Jin military forces occupied. The Song also made incursions into Jin territory and were another common problem for the Jin military. In addition, despite peaceful relations for decades, in 1210 Xi Xia began conducting raids. The Tanguts of Xi Xia were angry that their requests for help against the Mongols were casually brushed aside. Raids for plunder were the result.

The Jurchen yoke also fomented discontent among the Khitans, and prior to the invasion Genghis Khan had already arranged secret negotiations with several Khitan military commanders, many of whom agreed to support the Mongols. The Ongguts needed very little persuading to support the Mongols, and in the first invasion they immediately turned against their Jurchen masters. While Genghis Khan was certainly a master of military strategy and organization, his very considerable diplomatic skills have too often been overlooked. Much of this success in gaining allies was a result of his hard-earned reputation for being fair and trustworthy in negotiations and in carrying out the terms of any agreements he had sanctioned.

A new ruler came to the Jin throne in 1208 and a year later envoys came to the Mongols to inform them they had a new sovereign, for when Genghis Khan took control over the Kereits, he also acquired their vassal status to the Jin emperor. On this occasion, however, the Khan refused to recognize the new ruler in Zhongdu as his sovereign. Telling the Jin envoys that the new emperor was an idiot, Genghis Khan spat on the ground and rode off.[6] The Jin responded by strengthening some of their border forts, but they undertook no further actions to prepare for what should have been an obvious Mongol attack. Possibly the new emperor was dismissive of the Mongols, as some accounts have it. Challenges to the legitimacy of the emperor by others of the imperial family had also weakened the imperial court, and small-scale uprisings by Chinese peasants had become commonplace in several areas of northeast China.

In setting out to invade China in March of 1211, Genghis Khan proclaimed that the moral purpose of the campaign was to exact revenge for the execution of two Mongol leaders (and distant relatives of Genghis Khan) several decades earlier. The army that marched toward China was nearly 100,000 strong and moved along two main fronts. Genghis Khan personally commanded the central front whose first objective was acquisition of the region around the city of Datong. Mukali commanded the left front army along with his key subordinates Subodei and Jebe. Both front armies were divided into several subcommands, each with its own objectives. Ahead of the main forces rode 200–300 scouts and couriers who sought out sources of water, food, and fodder; looked for enemy concentrations and other sources of intelligence information; and kept the various units in communication with each other. Behind the army were vast numbers of carts with military provisions and weapons and spare horses. However, these supplies were to remain along the border until summoned. Once inside China the Mongols had no real supply lines and no rear guard. They intended to advance all the time and keep the Jin on the defensive.

The Mongols moved swiftly once in China, and the Jin response was slow and often confused. The Mongol advance from several points north left the Jin commanders puzzled as to how many of the enemy they were facing. The general Jebe particularly distinguished himself during this campaign. In an assault on one city along the strategic Juyong Pass (a steep hilly area of the Great Wall about thirty miles from present-day Beijing), Jebe engaged in a feigned retreat, even leaving many "wounded" Mongols on the battlefield. When the defending army left the city in pursuit, Jebe's command, now suddenly on the offensive, attacked with help from the "wounded" soldiers. The Jin army was utterly destroyed, allowing the Mongols to take control of the pass. A few weeks later, when confronting a large opposing Jin army, during the night Jebe sent several units quietly around to the Jin rear, where they picked off much of the rear guard. The rest of the rear guard fled in panic, causing chaos in the Jin camp. By the time of the battle the next day, even the Jin commander had run away, allowing the Mongols to score an impressive victory over a much large force.

During the course of the fighting many small and large units of Khitans and Chinese defected to the Mongols. Genghis Khan accepted all of them, even the Chinese infantry forces. From his experiences in Xi Xia, Genghis Khan realized that he would not be able to take major cities with only his cavalry, and he planned to utilize the Chinese experience with sieges. Yet, in the six months of campaigning in 1211, Genghis Khan had only limited success in taking walled and fortified cities. The Mongols took several small cities, sometimes as a result of defections by their defenders, but the largest cities remained just outside the Mongol grasp. The city of Datong, for example, held on through several brutal Mongol assaults. It was at Datong that Genghis Khan first employed the tactic of rounding up large numbers of the local population of women, children, and the elderly and forcing them to march in front of the Mongols as they assaulted the city. The defenders were forced to fire on fellow locals, including family members, while the Mongols forced them to take the brunt of the fire from the city.

The Mongol invading forces converged on the capital of Jin China in late September 1211. Zhongdu (present-day Beijing) was a massive, impressive city at that time. A wall nearly eighteen miles in length encircled the city, with a fifty-foot-wide base, nine hundred towers, and lines of deep moats around it. In addition, connected to the wall were four forts, each a mile square, with large garrisons defending them. Underground tunnels connected the network of fortresses and towers. The Mongols were aware that, although they had destroyed several Jin armies, the dynasty had not collapsed, and more Jin forces were forming up and preparing to attack them. Genghis Khan also understood that his Mongols were not able to invest such a large, well-fortified city. So he called in the supply carts, gathered up vast amounts of plunder and slaves, and withdrew back into Mongolia to prepare for the next year's campaigning season. He sent Jebe into Manchuria to take the region around the city of Liaodong and winter there. In the middle of winter, Jebe engaged in some brilliant campaigning, including a sudden attack on Liaodong as its residents celebrated Chinese Lunar New Year.[7]

The Mongol assaults devastated large areas of north China. Fields and orchards were laid waste, and hundreds of villages and towns destroyed. Those who survived suffered immense hunger and loss of property and loved ones. But the Jin proved resourceful, rebuilt their armies, and worked to rebuild their northern defenses. As destructive as the Mongol assault had been, millions of Chinese lived in these regions, and it was not possible to kill more than a portion of them. Unlike other Mongol campaigns, most of the slaughter was not systematic. A Mongol column would swoop in; defeat whatever defense forces were there to greet them; loot, burn, rape, and carry off prisoners; and then leave as swiftly as they had arrived. Genghis Khan left no garrison forces in China as he departed for Mongolia. The only exception was Jebe's force sent into Manchuria's Liaodong region, and this force was allied with a large number of Khitans who were fighting in their homeland.

When the attacks resumed in spring 1212, the Mongols were surprised to see that so many of the defenses had been repaired. The Jin greatly fortified the strategic Juyong Pass with many thousands of their best troops. They were not going to be fooled by a feigned retreat or other similar trickery. Genghis Khan called forth a Muslim merchant named Jafar who was very familiar with this region. He told Genghis Khan of a secret path through the mountainous region around the pass. Following Jafar, the Mongols quietly walked through the night behind the fortress and caught the over-confident garrison asleep. The attack was swift and brutal, and none of the defenders was allowed to live. As the remainder of the Mongol army marched through the pass, they came upon a defected Jurchen prince along with several thousand of his men who offered their services to the Mongol Khan. These men were brought into the army.

Rather than directly attack the heavily fortified Zhongdu, the Mongols launched large numbers of pillaging raids, deliberately destroying croplands to weaken and even ruin so far as possible the resource base of the Jin. Datong was besieged, but, when Genghis Khan suffered an arrow wound, the siege was called off and the Mongols once again returned to Mongolia.

The campaigns continued for two more years, with more devastation and death, and the Mongols acquired more experience in the one aspect of military affairs they were lacking, siege craft. During the attacks of 1213, each major Mongol army contained several Chinese units skilled in sieges. These units almost always were comprised of defected Chinese infantry who sought to join what was developing into the winning side. For some reason not clear in the sources, the Jin rarely took the initiative in the war, relying primarily on passive defense or slow-moving offensives that involved huge numbers of their own troops. There seemed to be little coordination or even cooperation between Jin military units, especially between the cavalry and the infantry. Genghis Khan took advantage of this, at times using sieges as little more than means to lure Jin armies to destruction. Mongol armies would lie in wait near besieged cities for Jin relief forces, and they would kill many thousands of Jin soldiers in these attacks. It also became clear by 1214 that Genghis Khan intended to once again radically alter traditional practices regarding nomadic success against China. In the past, nomadic armies might take and occupy regions along the frontiers of the steppe, but, most often, they would take the loot and plunder back to their homelands in Mongolia. Instead, Genghis Khan decided to occupy most of the territories his armies had plundered, even those deep into China. The Khan parceled out lands and people to both officers and men as rewards for good service.

By spring 1214, with the Mongols in possession of nearly all the lands north of the Yellow River, Genghis Khan felt prepared to institute a siege of Zhongdu itself. He and his officers had learned much about siege craft in the prior three years, and made some progress in their ability to besiege fortifications. Still, Zhongdu's defenses were massive and the Mongols, even with their tens of thousands of Chinese and Khitan auxiliaries, could not breech the walls. When disease broke out among the attackers, several of Genghis Khan's commanders called for a withdrawal. The Khan disagreed since he believed the Jin could not hold out much longer. He understood that there was much disorder and dissension among the Jin court. Indeed, earlier in the year one general killed the emperor and placed a nephew on the throne, intending to rule through this inexperienced and young puppet. But the general's power was short-lived as he, in turn, was killed by another Jin general, who now became the leading advisor to the young emperor. Intrigues were common and the Jin factions struggled as if their factional enemies were a bigger threat than the Mongols outside the gates. All this Genghis Khan knew, even if he was not fully aware of all the details. It was only a matter of time, he believed, before the city fell or the Mongols forced the Jin to negotiate and accept subordinate status. A message he sent to the Jin emperor stated: "All the places north of the [Yellow River] are mine, save [Zhongdu], which is all that remains in thy service.

Heaven has brought thee down to this impotence; were I to harass thee further I should dread Heaven's anger. Will thou treat my army well and satisfy my generals?"[8] This last statement, of course, referred to the loot and rapine that his soldiers wanted.

Genghis Khan, once again, proved very perceptive. By the end of summer 1214 the Jin emperor agreed to pay off the Mongols and accept subordinate status as "king" of Henan (one of the few provinces of north China still not under Mongol control) and a few other lands south of the Yellow River. The Jin ceded most of northern China and Manchuria outright to the Mongols. The Jin paid the Mongols with three thousand horses, five hundred boys and five hundred girls as slaves, and all the gold and silk the Mongols could carry in their carts. The Jin emperor also gave his daughter, reputedly the most beautiful woman in the world, in marriage to Genghis Khan.

Led by Genghis Khan, most of the Mongol army left the Zhongdu area and returned with their loot to Mongolia. Just outside the area of the Great Wall, a messenger galloped up to Genghis Khan and informed him that the Jin emperor and nearly all of his court had left Zhongdu and sought to take refuge in Kaifeng, the southern capital of the Jin. This enraged Genghis Khan, who believed it signaled the Jin's intention to dissolve their agreement and attempt to retake their territories. While much of the loot was sent on into Mongolia, Genghis Khan ordered the main army to double back with him. He also sent messengers to Mukali, then campaigning in Manchuria, to meet with him outside Zhongdu. Thus, Genghis Khan prepared to resume a midwinter siege, though Mukali would not arrive until the winter of 1214–1215.

The Khan sent a Mongol army directly to Kaifeng to attempt to catch the Jin emperor or at least his main army before they could take refuge in the city. The attempt was unsuccessful, so the Mongols initiated a siege of the city. A Jin relief force was sent from Zhongdu to the city and was defeated before it arrived. In fact, the Chinese commander and his officers were in the midst of a bout of hard drinking when the Mongols surprised them with their attack. After the defeat of this relief force, several Khitan units that had been part of the remaining Jin army defected to the Mongols and Genghis Khan assigned them to assist Mukali in his campaign to complete the conquest of Manchuria. Another force was sent under Subodei to take Korea.

With several thousand Mongols and Khitans, Subodei led several raiding expeditions into Korea. Rather than the outright conquest of Korea, the Mongols' main purpose was to secure their flank as they fought in China. After destruction of farmland and towns and massacres of the population, the Korean court accepted Mongol sovereignty and promised to send troops to assist in the conquest of Manchuria.

Genghis Khan designed the first assaults by the Mongols on the Manchurian region to weaken the Jin, neutralize the lands to the east of Mongolia, and take lands useful for raising horses. In fact, this final reason was more important than the others, as the Mongols relied on a steady supply of horses for their military forces. Raids in 1213 met with not only successful plundering expeditions but also new allies. A Khitan general broke from service to the Jin and offered to serve the Mongols with his several-thousand-strong cavalry force. Genghis Khan agreed to name him "king of Liaodong" if he proved useful. In 1214 when Mukali was sent to subdue Manchuria, this "king of Liaodong" proved to be very helpful indeed.

The Khitan defector impressed on Mukali the importance of taking the Manchurian capital of Liaoyang—which had also been the original capital of the Jurchens' territory. It housed the major Jin military force in Manchuria as well as maintaining enormous supplies of uniforms, weapons, and carts. Mukali's forces took the city surprisingly easily. They had learned that a new Khitan general was arriving to take command of the city. Mukali's men surprised and captured this new general and his aides. The Khitan defector took the commission of appointment, rode into the city, and convinced the leaders that he was the new commander. Once he and his men were put in charge, he opened the gate to the Mongols. As most of the garrison members were actually Khitans, they were allowed to join the Mongols.

In an assault on another city, Mukali was able to utilize the tactic that had worked so well in the siege of Volohai: hundreds of birds and cats were set on fire and sent into the city, causing it to catch fire and burn down. By March 1215, Mukali had secured nearly all of Manchuria and marched down to meet Genghis Khan outside the walls of Zhongdu.

The Mongol assault on Zhongdu was relentless, and many thousands of Chinese troops were used to ensure a firm siege. One Jin military commander successfully escaped before the siege was complete, and yet another despaired of success and committed suicide. As the Mongols took the outer four forts one by one, the interior of the city erupted in chaos and confusion. Fires and looting were rampant, and famine killed many by early May. After a Jin relief force was destroyed, it was clear the city could hold out no longer. The Mongols accomplished the final assault that captured the city very quickly.

When the Mongols rode into Zhongdu, the sack of the city was terrible to behold. For several days the Mongols set loose and devastated the city. Thousands were slaughtered and raped, and allegedly 60,000 women and girls committed suicide rather than allow themselves to be ravished by the Mongol soldiers. Caravans with thousands of carts hauled loot to Mongolia for weeks, and the fires started in the city reportedly lasted for over a month. The Mongols finally left Zhongdu with their last carts full of plunder when the stench of dead bodies became too much, even for these men accustomed to large-scale death. Even years later, travelers reported the area around the city was littered with the skulls of those killed.

Surprisingly, the capture of Zhongdu and the devastation of the lands of northern China did not end the war. Even while looting took place in Zhongdu, the Jin court in Kaifeng sent another relief force. The Mongols intercepted this force, and the whole unit was slaughtered. Nearly the whole of northern China was devastated. Enormous tracts of cropland were burned, flooded, or otherwise destroyed. Hundreds of villages, towns, and cities were leveled and destroyed. Many more emptied as a result of the deadly diseases that always accompany such death and destruction. In some cases, the Mongols forced whole populations to leave an area. They joined the millions of newly homeless wandering throughout the land, looking for food and security. Constant streams of people clogged the road and waterways going south, away from the dreaded Mongols. Banditry became the leading occupation after scavenging, and there was a tremendous societal breakdown.

In the winter of 1215–16, the only Mongol forces in the former Jin empire were in Manchuria and outside of Zhongdu. The Jin court in Kaifeng, showing amazing resilience, sought to recover its position and reconstruct its empire. By summer 1216 the Jin recovered several provinces and agricultural production resumed in formerly devastated lands. The Song to the south and the Xi Xia to the west attacked and took territories, but the reformed Jin army successfully recovered these lands. The Jin did not directly attack the Mongols' garrisons, yet Genghis Khan became determined to completely conquer the lands of north China and eliminate the Jin for good. To this end he assigned the task to the successful Mukali, giving him two Mongol tümen, about 60,000 Khitans and other allied soldiers, and an undetermined number of Chinese units.

The Mongols did not fully complete the task until 1234, and only then because the Mongols learned to pacify and rule lands that had been conquered.

Genghis Khan had learned the difference between destroying a land and conquering it. An empire such as Jin China with its tens of millions could not be taken with the traditional steppe nomad tactics. Still, massive slaughter and destruction of livelihood remained a major tactic in the conquest of China until Khubilai Khan, the grandson of Genghis Khan, launched the invasion of Song China in the 1250s.

As horrendous as the death and destruction of northern China was, Genghis Khan and his Mongol hordes made that look like a picnic compared with what they were preparing to do in the Muslim lands of Central Asia and Persia.

Destruction of the Khwarazmian Empire

G ENGHIS KHAN LOOKED to the empire of Khwarazm as his next target even while he was still engaged in battle in China. Khwarazm was a fairly new empire at the time it attracted Mongol attention. Indeed, in the early thirteenth century, the empire was still in the process of development. At its greatest extent, Khwarazm occupied much of Central Asia (parts of all the present-day "stans"), northeast Persia, and Afghanistan. The Khwarazm shah—or king—Muhammad Ala ad-Din, had grand ambitions, including a desire to replace the Abbasid caliph in Baghdad.[1] In the early 1200s, Muhammad Shah, with the assistance of Kara-Khitai, attacked the Ghurid rulers of Afghanistan, further enraging the caliph in Baghdad. After a major victory in battle in early 1206, Kara-Khitai forces returned to their homeland in the Tarim Basin region, and Muhammad Shah continued his efforts alone. By 1215 all of Afghanistan had been added to the Khwarazmian Empire.

Under the terms of the alliance with Kara-Khitai, technically, Muhammad Shah was the subordinate, but the 1206 victory encouraged Muhammad to act independently of his alliance—which probably contributed to the withdrawal of the Kara-Khitai forces. When the now-confident Muhammad conquered the cities of Samarkand and Bukhara in

1207, the rift was complete, as these two wealthy Silk Road trading cities were part of the Kara-Khitai's territory.

After taking control of Samarkand, Muhammad Shah let his troops loose to conduct a terrible slaughter of the Samarkand people. This brutal treatment can be traced back to Muhammad's daughter's marriage to the Turkish general in charge of Samarkand's defenses. The general—previously a friend and ally of Muhammad—took a liking to a younger and more attractive woman, at one point even requiring his wife (Muhammad's daughter) to serve this new object of his affection. The assault on Samarkand came from Muhammad's own designs, but the gratuitous slaughter grew out of his daughter's loud demands for vengeance.

In response to the assault on Samarkand, in 1210 Kara-Khitai attacked Khwarazm and had some small successes in repulsing the invaders from parts of its territory. To complicate matters even more, at this point the Naiman prince Küchlüg revolted against his Kara-Khitai sovereigns. After the Mongols defeated the Naiman in 1204, Küchlüg had fled with a number of his followers to Kara-Khitai. The Kara-Khitai ruler allowed Küchlüg and his people to settle in their lands and even appointed Küchlüg as commander of Naiman military forces defending the eastern frontier. This was a major mistake, for Küchlüg had ambitions beyond mere command of a few thousand border guards. Küchlüg's revolt was not an accident but part of an agreed alliance with Muhammad Shah. Already weakened by war with Khwarazm, Kara-Khitai fell to Küchlüg within a year, and he named himself ruler. In 1212 Muhammad Shah moved the Khwarazmian capital to Samarkand and gave himself the elevated title of "sultan."

Not long after this there was a falling out between the Khwarazm ruler and the new ruler of Kara-Khitai. Possibly Muhammad Shah looked to add the rest of Kara-Khitai to his empire or was insulted in some way by Küchlüg's apparent design to restore Khwarazm's subordinate relationship. Whatever the case, Muhammad Shah's conquests did not appear to be governed by any grand strategy, he sought out targets of opportunity, with an ultimate goal of replacing the caliph in Baghdad. The shah's moves against Kara-Khitai came at a time of seeming weakness in that land, for Küchlüg's coup had led many of the Uighur lands to shift their loyalty to Genghis Khan's Mongols. Yet, Küchlüg and his mainly Turkish military force were, with effort, able to repulse the Khwarazmian probes. However, in the process, the areas where combat took place suffered horribly.

Küchlüg would seem to be the perfect match for Muhammad Shah, having a similar personality, similar goals and ambitions, and equal incompetence when assessing the immediate world around him. While he must have possessed some skills in order to overthrow the rulers of Kara-Khitai, once in power he proceeded to alienate large numbers of his new subjects. Possibly under the influence of his wife, Küchlüg decided to impose religious conformity on the population and demanded that the predominantly Muslim population of Kara-Khitai renounce their faith for either his Nestorian Christianity or his wife's Buddhism. Protesting imams and Muslim scholars were crucified in front of their mosques.[2] At the same time, Küchlüg launched a surprise attack on a minor tribal chief near the border with the Mongols and killed him. This seemingly minor incident had historical consequences for the world, for that chief was a sworn subject of the Mongol chief, Genghis Khan.

While Genghis Khan did not follow some grand strategic plan, to conquer a large-scale empire, individual campaigns were often so meticulously planned that they do appear to be part of some larger scheme. The assault on Kara-Khitai fits this pattern well. Genghis Khan could not have been happy at the rising fortunes of his old Naiman enemy, Küchlüg. This land was now a potential threat to the Mongol empire and would have to be dealt with eventually—if Küchlüg did not attack first. Genghis Khan also keenly felt the direct assault on one who had pledged fealty to him. The preparations for the attack on Kara-Khitai followed the usual system of careful planning: Genghis Khan ordered detailed surveys of the social and political situation of the land, hired trustworthy guides familiar with the layout of the land, and detailed preparations for logistics and routes of march. But, when he proclaimed that his forces were marching in to Kara-Khitai in support of his aggrieved vassals, was this also an excuse to grab land?

In early 1218 Genghis Khan sent the general Jebe with roughly two tümen (twenty thousand men) to assault Küchlüg. This force met with quick success; Jebe's forces moved quickly to disrupt the small units of Naiman they faced. Küchlüg retreated with his main body of troops to the Kashgar region. In typical Mongol style, Jebe rapidly pushed on and, within a few weeks, had destroyed his opponents. Küchlüg himself was captured and beheaded.

Two related forces aided Jebe in this conquest. Once the Mongol invasion force had entered Kara-Khitai, internal revolts sprang up against Küchlüg throughout the land. Local Islamic leaders proclaimed the Mongols were liberators and called on the people to support them against the anti-Muslim Küchlüg and his Naiman. The Mongols knew of the religious ferment in Kara-Khitai, and from the first day of the invasion Jebe proclaimed a policy of religious tolerance. The anti-Muslim edicts were rescinded, and the Mongol troops showed remarkable discipline, demonstrating the successful training Genghis Khan had instilled in them. The invasion force committed very few acts of slaughter or destruction. Of course, this is only remarkable in the context of the Mongol reputation for ferocity and cruelty. The restraint exhibited in the Kara-Khitai invasions reminds us that discipline was a hallmark of Genghis Khan's training regimen and that Mongol cruelty and slaughter were military strategies and not inherent Mongol cultural characteristics. Tolerance and respect for the Kara-Khitai's people and property make for perfect strategies in this campaign and should not be seen as aberrations from "usual" Mongol practice.

The first military contact between Genghis Khan's Mongols and the Khwarazm Empire took place while the Mongols were involved in other operations. At the same time Genghis Khan sent Jebe to fight Kara-Khitai, he directed another force of about twenty thousand under Subodei and Genghis Khan's son Jöchi to attack the remaining Merkits. Traveling north and west along the Altai Mountains, they passed through Qarlaq lands. The Qarlaqs had voluntarily submitted to Genghis Khan a few years earlier; however, the commanders probably felt some nervousness in considering how sincere the Qarlaqs were in their supplication. Subodei need not have fretted, as the Qarlaqs not only allowed the Mongols to transit their lands but also provided scouts and intelligence on the Merkits. The actual location and flow of battles is not known, but in the end the Merkits were thoroughly subdued.

In chasing the fleeing remnants of the Merkit force, at one point the Mongols crossed into Khwarazm territory. When Muhammad Shah was informed, he sent a large force against the Mongols. Fighting was hard, and Subodei and his men slipped out at night and left Khwarazm. While it is

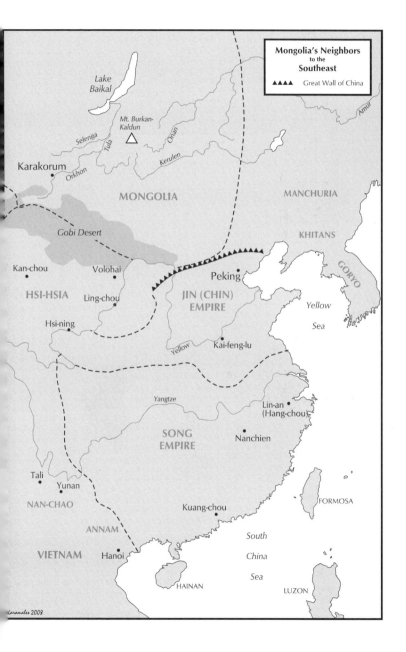

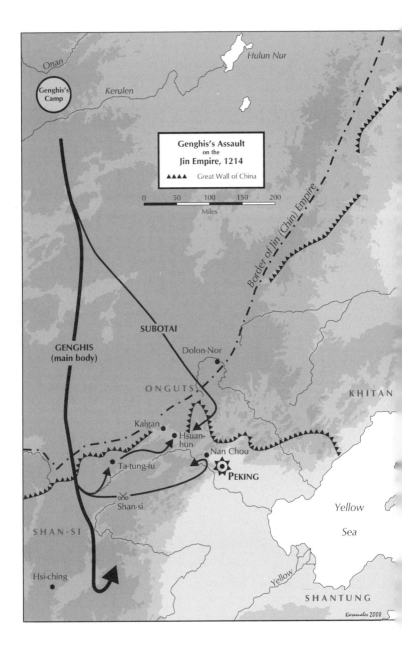

Onan

Hulun Nur

Kerulen

Genghis's
Camp

Genghis's Assault
on the
Jin Empire, 1214

▲▲▲▲ Great Wall of China

0   50   100   150   200
|___|___|___|___|___|
        Miles

Border of Jin (Chin) Empire

SUBOTAI

GENGHIS
(main body)

Dolon-Nor

ONGUTS

KHITAN

Kalgan

Hsuan-
hun

Nan Chou

Ta-tung-fu

PEKING

Shan-si

Yellow

SHAN-SI

Sea

Hsi-ching

Yellow

SHANTUNG

Karamales 2008

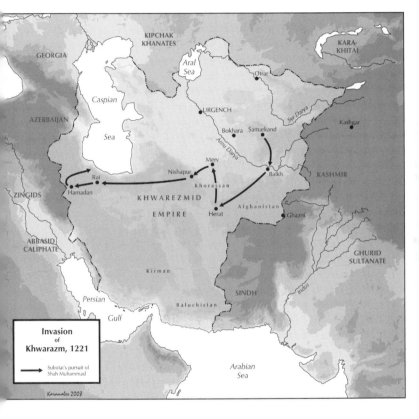

GEORGIA

KIPCHAK
KHANATES

KARA-
KHITAI

*Aral
Sea*

Caspian

Otrar

URGENCH

Sea

AZERBAIJAN

Bokhara Samarkand

Amu Darya

Syr Darya

Kashgar

Rai

Merv

Nishapur

Balkh

KASHMIR

ZINGIDS

Hamadan

Khorassan

KHWAREZMID

Afghanistan

EMPIRE

Herat

Ghazni

ABBASID
CALIPHATE

GHURID
SULTANATE

Kirman

Indus

SINDH

Baluchistan

Persian

Gulf

*Arabian
Sea*

| Invasion |
| of |
| Khwarezm, 1221 |

Subotai's pursuit of
Shah Muhammad

Karamdas 2008

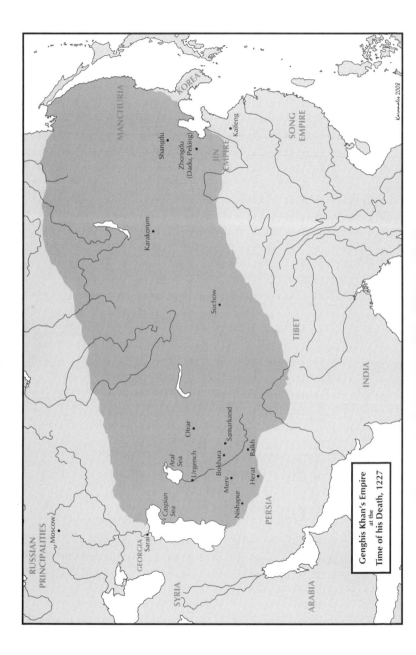

Genghis Khan's Empire
at the
Time of his Death, 1227

reported that the shah was impressed with the fighting abilities of the Mongols, his relatively swift "victory" might have led him to underestimate the Mongols. Such an interpretation would help explain some of Muhammad Shah's later odd military decisions when the Mongols invaded his land in force. For Genghis Khan, the Merkits' defeat and confirmation of the Qarlaqs' loyalty were the most important benefits of the expedition. Now when war with Muhammad Shah came, he no longer had to worry about attacks to his left and rear.

The actual war to take Kara-Khitai was, in fact, quite anticlimactic. The realm fell quickly to Mongol forces, which has led many to see it as merely an opening to the true war to take Khwarazm. However, the evidence does not support such a reading, especially since at that time, Genghis Khan did not plan the invasion as an initial phase of a larger war against Khwarazm. But it is not clear what Genghis Khan's early intentions were toward Khwarazm.[3] Most likely he aimed to, at minimum, weaken a possible rival and keep the lines of trade through the Silk Road open. Subodei's earlier clash with Khwarazm was minor and accidental, a consequence of his attack on the Merkits, and did not appear to play any role in later decisions regarding that land. There were later stories that the caliph in Baghdad had secretly contacted Genghis Khan to request an alliance against their common enemy, Muhammad Shah. According to the tales, the caliph sent his ambassador with the request tattooed on his scalp. This scenario is unlikely, but not impossible, as the caliph's agents were aware of a powerful force on the eastern borders of the Khwarazm Empire. In addition, Jebe's very swift subjugation of Kara-Khitai led to concerns in the Khan's camp that Jebe might consider himself independent and possibly even a rival to Genghis Khan. Jebe protested that he was loyal to the Khan and even sent a gift of one thousand horses of the same type that Jebe had shot out from under Genghis Khan, reminding the Great Khan of the incident that led to Jebe's oaths of loyalty. Still, sending the successful general on further campaigns against the powerful Khwarazm Empire would keep him occupied regardless of possible questions about his loyalty.

In 1218 Genghis Khan sent a message to the Khwarazm ruler that asked for friendly trade relations between the two empires. In his request he wrote:

I know your power and the vast extent of your empire. I have the greatest desire to live in peace with you. I shall regard you as my son. For your part, you must know that I have conquered northern China and subdued all the tribes of the north. You know that my country is a swarm of warriors, a mine of silver, and that I have no need to covet further dominions. We have an equal interest in encouraging trade between our subjects.[4]

The shah was not amused at being referred to as the "son" of someone he considered an infidel barbarian, but he agreed to discuss relations.

Jebe separately sent envoys assuring the shah the Mongol attack on Kara-Khitai was not ultimately aimed at Khwarazm. Genghis Khan also sought out merchants from Khwarazm and assured them the Mongols wanted only open trade relations. The same year a large caravan of merchants from Mongol territories—along with a personal emissary from Genghis Khan—entered Khwarazm and one of its major trading cities, Otrar. The city's governor, suspecting Mongol spies were among the merchants, had them executed and confiscated their goods. There is some dispute over whether the governor took this action on his own or on the orders of Muhammad Shah. But the execution order was not completely carried out, as one man survived and returned to Mongol territory to relate what had happened. Outraged, Genghis Khan sent an embassy directly to Muhammad Shah. The shah shaved off the men's beards and sent them back humiliated. Secluding himself for three days, Genghis Khan communed with Tengri to prepare himself for the coming campaign.

As he took steps to organize his armies for another major military expedition, his then-favorite wife Yesui (a Tatar woman Genghis spared from the general slaughter order) reminded him, as he was getting older and about to embark on more fighting, that he should name his successor. Genghis Khan does not come down to us in the records as a strong family man, and, indeed, he seems to have never developed close personal bonds with any of his sons as they grew up. Certainly he relied on and trusted them as at least nominal commanders of his major armies, but only Tolui showed promise as a leader worthy of comparison to generals such as Subodei, Mukali, and Jebe. Still, while Genghis Khan broke many steppe traditions, he was aware that the only real hope of Mongol unity after his passing would come from the selection of one of his sons as leader. And, he could only choose from the sons of his first wife, Börte.

Calling his sons, advisors, and primary generals together, Genghis Khan called on his sons to speak, beginning with the eldest, Jöchi. The second eldest, Chaghatai, leaped up and demanded that his father exclude Jöchi from the succession because of his suspicious birth. The two brothers were barely prevented from coming to blows when their father proposed a compromise. While the evidence suggests he preferred Tolui—and steppe tradition did not necessarily favor the oldest son—Genghis Khan was more concerned with preventing a possible civil war among his sons, another steppe tradition. Whether Genghis Khan cleverly set up the sons for this confrontation or he took advantage of what was unfolding before him is not clear. However, he gained all his sons' approval for him to be succeeded by the third son, Ögödei, thus preventing certain civil war if he had chosen either Jöchi or Chaghatai. Ögödei also had a reputation for being more intelligent and diplomatic than his brothers. His rule after Genghis Khan's death in 1227 would not have disappointed his father, though his later downfall came not from internecine strife but rather his further well-deserved reputation as a lover of strong drink.

To further emphasize the point that leadership in the new Mongolia was dependent primarily on skill and merit, according to the *Secret History*, Genghis Khan decreed:

> I've appointed one of my sons to rule. If all of you respect this decree then all will go well. And if the descendants of Ögödei are so empty of bravery that wrapped in sweet grass an ox won't even eat them, wrapped in rich fat a dog won't even smell them, then some other one of my descendants will be found to succeed him.[5]

With a successor chosen, Genghis Khan turned his attention back to his next campaign. A brief survey of the opposing forces would lead one to conclude Muhammad Shah clearly held the upper hand. The land of Khwarazm was not much larger than that of the Mongols but contained vastly more people, including numerous hardy Turkish warriors. Muhammad himself was a highly educated Turkish warrior who had demonstrated a great deal of skill in creating and managing this large empire.

The two key secrets to the shah's success were the many thousands of Turkish soldiers who formed the core of his large army and the support of the various traditional elites of the region. He gave those who cooperated a good deal of autonomy, while those who opposed him were brutalized. As noted earlier, Muhammad Shah also had grand ambitions of replacing the caliph in Baghdad and possibly a conquest of China. Mongol war on the Jin had disrupted those plans, but a number of spies kept the shah informed about the situation in China, and they especially included information on Mongol tactics, strategies, strengths, and weaknesses. From these reports he concluded that the Mongols were nearly unbeatable in the field but lacked the skills to take well-fortified cities.

Once one digs a little deeper into the strategic situation within Khwarazm, Muhammad Shah's advantages do not look quite so forbidding. The vast army—reputedly numbering over four hundred thousand—was mostly unreliable, and many of the core Turkish units were mainly mercenary forces, loyal as long as they were allowed to exploit the populations under their control. This exploitation, both economic and physical, led to a great deal of discontent among the people. Muhammad's support among the elites of the region was also very unreliable and needed constant reinforcing. Muhammad Shah could not depend on more than a few of his commanders, in marked contrast to Genghis Khan's relationships with his generals. It is worth repeating that Genghis Khan's insistence on commanders of proven merit—regardless of social status—led not only to better leadership and unity of command but better loyalty as well. Genghis Khan knew of Khwarazm's many weaknesses, and he exploited them.

Thus, Khwarazm was a very large empire that was, to a great degree, decentralized. Muhammad Shah spent most of his years in power expanding the territory of his empire and not enough time consolidating his rule. In the years leading up to the war, the shah ordered a tripling of the taxes and collected revenue in advance in order to further fortify the main cities of the empire and to enlarge and strengthen his military forces. Whether this was decreed in anticipation of war against the Mongols or against others is not clear, but the new impositions led to several revolts by the populace, even in Samarkand, the capital.

In 1218, aware of the Mongol intention to attack, Muhammad Shah called a meeting of his top commanders and advisors in order to devise a strategy to meet the Mongol challenge. His son and, by far, best field commander, Jalal ad-Din, advised striking hard at the Mongols as soon as they came near the Syr Darya River. Once stopped, the Mongols should not be allowed to rest, he advised, but kept constantly on the defensive. This was not the advice followed by Muhammad Shah. Instead, he decided to divide his large force into many garrisons, and he posted them in newly fortified main cities. The largest armed force was to be kept on the west bank of the Amu Darya River. The shah did not trust his commanders to effectively carry out a major battle early in the fight; or, if they did and were successful, he was concerned that such a commander would immediately become a rival to his own authority. He was also influenced by reports he had received of Mongol fighting in northern China. Let the Mongols bloody themselves by battering uselessly against my fortified cities, reasoned Muhammad Shah, and then we'll pounce on them as they limp back to Mongolia.

The war the Khwarazm shah expected was not the war he received. Genghis Khan and his commanders learned a lot from the war in China, and they had quite accurate reports on the true situation within Khwarazm. During the spring and especially summer of 1219, Genghis Khan organized his forces and planned his strategy. In addition to a main force of Mongols, Uighurs, Qarlaqs, Khitans, and several thousand other Turkish warriors joined the army. Training was constant, with several great hunts used to improve coordination and cooperation among the various units. While we do not know if Genghis Khan was aware of the decisions made at Muhammad Shah's strategy meetings, he certainly obtained intelligence of the disposition of the main Khwarazm units. That Muhammad Shah intended to shelter most of his toughest warriors behind the walls of fortified cities was clear enough. But the wars in Xi Xia and Jin China showed the Mongols the futility of sending cavalry against fortifications. So, for this campaign Genghis Khan incorporated many thousands of Chinese warriors along with an array of siege engines, including fire rockets, mobile towers with retractable ladders, and huge crossbows that fired enormous flaming arrows. Genghis Khan selected these fighters from among the many Chinese units that had defected during the war in China. As noted in chapter 5, they learned that while Mongol discipline could be fierce and brutal, the Mongols did indeed richly reward successful allies.

When the Mongol army marched into Khwarazm it arrived with a large array of siege engines and many men experienced in siege craft. While the Khwarazm army was enormous, it was also divided into a large number of smaller units defending a variety of strategic spots, cities, and other fortifications. The ironic result was that the Mongols could usually expect to outnumber their opponents during specific encounters.

In the fall of 1219 the Mongol army of about 150,000–200,000 men approached Khwarazm. Genghis Khan had divided the army into four main divisions: three divisions were under the command of his sons and advanced toward cities along the Syr Darya, and the fourth was under his personal command. As a result of the excellent Mongol intelligence network, Genghis Khan was not surprised when the Khwarazmian army failed to sally forth and contest the Mongol advance.

Otrar, the city where the Mongol ambassadors had been defiled, was the first target. Forces under the combined command of Ögödei and Chaghatai quickly surrounded this city (located in the south of present-day Kazakhstan) in late 1219. The army brought up the Chinese siege machinery, and the city was besieged for five months before falling. This was one of the longest sieges of the whole campaign, but, even so, it was much shorter than many of the sieges the Mongols conducted in the invasion of China. Genghis Khan and his commanders had indeed learned well from their China experience and added Chinese siege craft to their own inventory of military abilities.

Otrar's fairly sturdy and long-lasting defense is not so hard to fathom. The governor knew what his fate would be at the hands of the Mongols and squelched all talk of negotiation. As food ran out and the situation became progressively more hopeless, one of the Turkish commanders decided to slip out of the city with his force of thousands of warriors. The Mongols caught this force and the commander offered to serve them. They treated the commander and his men well at first, and the Mongols accepted them into their ranks. However, after providing a detailed description of the defenses of the city, the whole unit was executed to the man. Genghis Khan had instructed his subordinates that no Turkish defectors were to be accepted into Mongol ranks once the war began. The exact reasons for this policy are still debated, but it was not relaxed until after Khwarazm was destroyed.[6]

With their newly acquired knowledge of the types and locations of the defenses, the Mongols quickly took the city. The governor and several thousand of his remaining men took refuge in a fortified citadel within the city and held out for weeks longer. According to accounts of the battle, when the defenders ran out of arrows they began to toss roof tiles down upon the Mongols. When the Mongols finally won the citadel, they executed all the prisoners, and the governor suffered a particularly painful death—molten silver was allegedly poured into his eyes and ears.

Genghis Khan considered the capture of Samarkand, Khwarazm's capital located between the Syr Darya and Amu Darya rivers, a primary goal, but the Mongols did not approach it directly. While three of the Mongol divisions were picking off the cities that lay along the Syr Darya, Genghis Khan and his son Tolui took the fourth division to the north and crossed the frozen Syr Darya River in February 1220. The immediate goal was Bukhara, near the Amu Darya River. Friendly Turkoman tribesmen aided the Mongols in their march through sometimes very harsh and dry terrain and guided them to the less dangerous pathways. The fourth division mercilessly sacked towns along the way to provide provisions for its men. The Mongols achieved complete surprise when they swooped down on the city of Bukhara. Genghis Khan had not brought many of his Chinese siege units with him, hoping surprise would give him the edge. In this he was mostly correct, but Bukhara's defenders fought fiercely for two days. Mongol assaults were relentless, and the major portion of the Turkish defense force decided to risk a direct sortie from the city. They succeeded in causing temporary disarray among the Mongols and probably should have taken the opportunity to flee. Instead, feeling confident, the Turks did not leave but continued their attack. The Mongols regrouped, counterattacked, and slew every single one of the enemy. The city lay open, but the remaining few hundred defenders—much like in Otrar—barricaded themselves in the citadel. This, too, was taken, and the prisoners were slaughtered.

The Mongols continued to use propaganda as a weapon in their conquest of Khwarazm. Upon entering the conquered city, Genghis Khan ordered that Islamic clerics tend to the Mongols' horses, while he himself marched to the grand mosque. The wealthy, powerful, and other elites of the city were forced to gather below as Genghis Khan harangued them from the pulpit. Using language atuned to his Muslim audience, the Khan proclaimed that the leading people of Khwarazm had committed vast sins and that he and his Mongols were "the scourge of God" come to punish them for these sins. Absolute obedience and service to the Mongols would allow them to cleanse themselves. Resistance was futile and would be brutally punished.

After this harangue, he got down to business, ordering Bukhara's wealthy to point out where they had hidden their treasures. After a raucous victory party held in the grand mosque, Genghis Khan ordered the whole population to leave the city, taking nothing but the clothes they wore. The Mongols then proceeded to thoroughly loot the city, and those who were caught hiding were killed on the spot. This new type of methodical plunder represented yet another lesson learned from the Chinese campaigns, especially the disorganized and destructive (for the Mongols) sack of Zhongdu. After the Mongols took their loot, they set the city aflame, leaving only one or two buildings to survive the destruction. The general population was then allowed to reenter the now-devastated city. The Mongols then ordered thousands of the residents to carry the loot and supplies as the Mongol army marched towards its next target, Samarkand.

In March 1220 Genghis Khan led the fourth division of Mongols towards Samarkand, leaving a small garrison force in the area of Bukhara. The Mongols forcibly took thousands of artisan families to be resettled in Mongolia, and they forced many more thousands to accompany them as servants and conscripts for the next campaign. Samarkand's defenders, like those in Bukhara, were surprised by the appearance of the Mongol army from behind. Upon his arrival, Genghis Khan surrounded the city. However, Samarkand was a much larger city than Bukhara, with over forty thousand soldiers in its garrison, deep lines of fortification, and large stores of food and water. In order to make the army seem more imposing than it was, Genghis Khan ordered the Bukhara captives aligned to appear as if they were in military formations, complete with banners and flags. This deception was enough to keep the defenders within the city rather than attack. Two days later, Chaghatai and Ögödei arrived with their divisions; Genghis Khan decided to kept these divisions intact, rather than join the siege, in order to serve as a reserve against any relief forces sent by Muhammad Shah to aid Samarkand. Spies had reported the main Khwarazmian army was on its way. In fact, the main army remained on the west bank of the Amu Darya, and Muhammad Shah sent a force of only twenty thousand to the relief of Samarkand. The Mongols quickly routed this force. A Turkish force of a few thousand negotiated with the Mongols to come over to their side, and Genghis Khan accepted this offer.

The fight for Samarkand began on the third day of the siege. The defenders repulsed Mongol assaults but at tremendous cost. The defenders even sallied out once themselves, allegedly behind a line of war elephants. But the Mongols stopped this sortie and forced the defenders back into the city. On the morning of the fourth day, several wealthy and powerful leaders of the city came out and promised to open the gates of the city in return for their own safety and the safety of their families. This was granted, and the Mongols gained entrance to the city. The remainder of Samarkand's military garrison retreated to the citadel while a number of the population (mostly visiting merchants and others not native to the region and thus fearing death if they surrendered) formed themselves into military units and attacked the Mongols. A horrendous slaughter followed.

The bulk of the population heeded the Muslim religious authorities who ordered cooperation with the Mongols, who now began their usual thorough—and brutal—sifting through the spoils of war. Those under the protection of the clerics who had ordered cooperation had their lives—though not their property—spared. All others who were not so designated were cut down on the spot. The Mongols needed only one more day to take the citadel, which they did by using pots of naphtha to set the fortification on fire. Most of the defenders burned to death, and, of the survivors, no prisoners were taken but executed on the spot. In a reprise of their plunder of Bukhara, the Mongols ordered the remaining population out of the city while it was being looted. Roughly fifty thousand people were under the protection of the Muslim clerics, and the Mongols kept their word to spare them, though they relocated many artisan and scribal families to Mongolia. The Mongols also killed the members of the Turkish units that had defected early in the fighting, as they considered them to be untrustworthy men who would shift loyalties during battle.

The city of Samarkand was devastated. The city had a highly intricate series of canals that provided water for irrigation, drinking, and the production of colorful dyes for which the city was famous. The Mongols literally obliterated the canals during and even after the siege. While

Bukhara would become a center of Central Asian trade within a few years, Samarkand took decades to recover and really never again enjoyed the sort of wealth and influence it had before the Mongols descended upon it.

Samarkand's capture proved to be the key battle of the war, though at the time this was not understood. The token efforts to support Samarkand's defense had weakened the shah's forces, and the seeming ease with which the Mongols had taken this capital city sent waves of fear through the remaining ranks of Khwarazm's soldiers. Muhammad Shah's strategy had been shown to be tragically wrong, but it was too late for him to regroup to make a serious defense of the rest of his empire.

But the war, of course, was not over; in fact, the worst devastation to be inflicted on a civilized land by the Mongols was only now just beginning. At this time, Genghis Khan sent an order to Korea for his subjects there to provide the Mongols with an enormous quantity of paper (Korean paper-making had a high reputation among the Mongols). He had a decree copied out in Uighur script and distributed throughout the remaining lands of Khwarazm:

> O commandants, officials, and people! Know ye that Heaven has given me the Empire of the earth, both the east and the west of it. Those who submit will be spared; woe to those who resist, they will be slaughtered with their children, and wives, and dependents. . . . Think not to meet water with fire, or to trust in your walls, or the numbers of those who defend them. If ye try to escape utter ruin will seize you.[7]

Mongol forces moved northward to the old Khwarazm capital of Urgench. Here Genghis Khan left his sons Jöchi, Chaghatai, and Ögödei to take that city with about fifty thousand men. This proved to be more difficult than expected, especially after the rapid destruction of a string of cities along the Syr Darya. Urgench's defenders—a mixed force of Persians, Turks, and others—fought hard, but quarrels between Jöchi and Chaghatai were the main cause underlying the slow progress. Actual command of the units was in the hands of trusted generals, but the sons of the Khan set the main strategy. Units from within the city gained several victories because of a loose siege. While the brothers quarreled and failed to keep their attention on the siege, Turkish units managed to escape.

When the siege engines had done their work and breached the walls of the city, Jöchi ordered a massed Mongol charge. The ensuing fighting was fierce and went street-by-street and often house-by-house. The Mongol soldiers were not accustomed to street fighting and suffered large casualties. After almost six months, Ögödei uncharacteristically stepped in and put an end to this seemingly endless, small-scale fighting. Pulling the Mongols out of the city, he ordered the whole place first flooded with the waters of the Amu Darya and then the remainder torched. Those who managed to escape the flames were slaughtered.

Jöchi was reportedly greatly angered by his brother's actions. The Khan had promised him the lands of Khwarazm, and he had intended to make Urgench his capital. The ruins he now beheld could not make a capital city, and he loudly criticized his brother for destroying it. Jöchi's very public denunciation of Ögödei's actions made Genghis Khan unsettled in his views of his eldest son. Indications are that he believed Jöchi was not only the source of most of the sibling contention, but also that he would surely break away from his brothers once his father was gone. Therefore, according to some reports, in 1223 Genghis Khan ordered the secret poisoning death of Jöchi, ending the sibling rivalry that he feared would tear his empire apart.[8]

Earlier, in 1220, while Genghis Khan left with one Mongol force for Afghanistan, he split up the remaining divisions of the Mongol army to complete the conquest of Khorasan in the eastern regions of Persia and to capture the shah. Muhammad Shah had fled Samarkand just ahead of the Mongol armies and had similarly just escaped capture at Urgench. For a while he made Nishapur his capital. His last line of defense was in the Zagros Mountains, to which he retreated and turned over execution of the war to his son, Jalal ad-Din. Genghis Khan's son, Tolui, was formally in charge of the efforts in Khorasan and was to catch Muhammad Shah. In these efforts he more than lived up to his reputation as the most cruel and destructive of Genghis Khan's commanders.

The Khan instructed his units tasked with the capture of Muhammad Shah to bypass any town or city that submitted and offered no resistance. One of the most militarily successful generals on this mission, Toguchar, disobeyed these orders and delayed his advance by plundering several of the submitted towns. When word of this reached Genghis Khan he immediately had Toguchar demoted to a common soldier but was dissuaded from having Toguchar executed only because he was married to the Khan's daughter.

The only time the shah actually met the Mongols in battle, at Hamadan in 1220, his twenty thousand soldiers were routed by a much smaller force under Jebe's command. The shah fled to an island in the Caspian Sea, where he died in December of that year apparently of complications from pneumonia. Jalal ad-Din was formally the new ruler of Khwarazm, but actually most of the land fell into the hands of either local military governors or other traditional local elites.

Within one year, nearly the whole of what had been the Khwarazm Empire was in the hands of the Mongols. While some garrisons fought bravely and forced the Mongols into sometimes-costly sieges, most fell in battle swiftly. The Mongols were not always scrupulous about adhering to their promises of safety for those lands that submitted without a fight. In some cases, the Mongols merely circled back after a battle to slaughter the inhabitants of cities they had once bypassed.

Mongol atrocities in the western lands of Khwarazm were ferocious. In one case the city of Zava had bought safety with a large amount of tribute and was to be spared a Mongol sack.[9] As the Mongol army marched past, many of the citizens climbed to the tops of the walls and taunted them, after which Genghis Khan ordered his force to return, plunder, slaughter the inhabitants, and burn down the city. Forces under Genghis Khan's personal command took the city of Balkh in late 1220. In addition to the usual slaughter of the population, the Mongols captured the shah's mother. While all of her servants and accompanying family members were killed, this powerful and influential woman was spared but sent back to Mongolia where she was forced to be a servant to one of Genghis Khan's wives. When the ancient Persian city of Merv fell in early 1221, Tolui ordered the whole population massacred except for about four hundred artisans —a common Mongol practice. Artisans were often sent back to Mongolia. To enjoy the "show," he perched himself on a hill, sitting in a golden throne. (A small Turkish tribe that resided and grazed in the vicinity of Merv fled just ahead of the Mongols. They were given sanctuary in the Seljuk lands of Anatolia and formed the foundations of what would later become the Ottoman Empire.)

The city of Nishapur suffered a fate even worse than the others, if that can be imagined. Several groups of Mongols came to Nishapur to assess the situation and the residents there gave them provisions but refused to surrender the city. When members of the garrison left to gain further support and to collect additional information about the land, they were caught and executed. When the Mongols learned that for a few weeks in summer 1220 the shah had made Nishapur his temporary capital, they decided to take and "punish" the city. Toguchar—the demoted son-in-law of Genghis Khan—had been pardoned and placed in command of the assaulting troops. Nishapur's defenders were able to repulse the Mongols, and during the battle Toguchar was shot and killed by an arrow. Two months later, Tolui and Jebe arrived with a larger Mongol force and, using twenty large catapults, battered down the walls of the city. Angry about the death of his brother-in-law, Tolui ordered extermination for the whole population of the city, including even the cats and dogs. The army beheaded the inhabitants and placed their skulls into separate piles for men, women, and children. When the entire population was destroyed, the Mongols tore down the city, burned it, ploughed up the land, and imposed a ban on reentering it.

Meanwhile, Jalal ad-Din had retreated to Ghazni, in Afghanistan, and raised another army. This army, under the command of Shigi-Khutuqu (the adopted son of Genghis Khan and later, according to some, the author of *Secret History*) confronted him in a battle near Kabul but was forced to retreat. This was the only pitched battle the Mongols lost in the whole war for Khwarazm. Genghis Khan responded to this loss by leading a force of some forty thousand to Afghanistan. Jalal ad-Din's victory over the Mongols had led to dissent within his ranks, and many of his conscript Afghan soldiers began to terrorize Ghazni's population. On paper he had over sixty thousand men, but only a few thousand Turkish warriors could be relied on. When informed that Genghis Khan was fast approaching Ghazni, Jalal ad-Din left the city. The two sides met in a hard-fought battle along the west bank of the Indus River in December 1221. Jalal ad-Din proved to be a much more formidable and capable commander than any other that the Mongols faced in Khwarazm, but the Mongols cut his soldiers down, and he only escaped by dashing across the Indus River on his horse. Genghis Khan pointed to Jalal ad-Din as an admirable man of bravery and let him go. He was given refuge in the Delhi Sultanate and tried for several more years to raise an army to push the Mongols out and recover his lost lands.

Genghis Khan marched back and forth through the Punjab region (in present-day Pakistan) as well as Afghanistan, ordering the complete destruction of both Ghazni and Herat. Scholars have long speculated about why he did not proceed into the Delhi Sultanate's lands and continue the conquests. But as spring turned into summer, the Mongols found the heat and terrain of the Indus valley too oppressive, so they decided to return to Afghanistan. In addition, with Khwarazm now effectively destroyed, Genghis Khan may have wished to punish Xi Xia for its failure to assist him. The Mongols remained in Afghanistan until the summer of 1223.

When Genghis Khan finally returned to Mongolia that summer, he was accompanied by a long caravan filled with the loot he had acquired on campaign. While the Mongols still conducted operations against the remaining cities and forces under commanders bold enough (or ignorant enough) to contest the Mongols for rule of the lands of Khorasan and the Caucasus, the war was essentially complete. The death and destruction were nearly incalculable. The Mongols utterly destroyed Khorasan's vast and intricate series of irrigation works, canals, and reservoirs, leading not only to immediate death and destruction on a massive scale, but to a famine that lasted for years in a land where agriculture depended on these systems. In some of the Muslim areas the Mongols especially aimed to kill religious leaders and scholars, but they did not target them because of their religion. A strategy designed to demoralize a population and decapitate the leadership motivated Mongol actions. For the same reasons, they killed or enslaved large numbers of the wealthy and aristocratic families of the region. Once a territory was firmly in their hands, the traditional Mongol religious tolerance reasserted itself. On his way back to Mongolia, Genghis Khan decreed that all holy men and religious figures, regardless of religion, were to be exempt from taxes. Indeed, he also sought out Muslim scholars to serve the Mongols as administrators in the cities of the newly conquered lands. And in summer 1223, Genghis Khan decreed that any Turkish tribe from the lands of the former Khwarazm could now petition to become part of Mongol military service.

Unlike the early campaigns in northern China, from the start Genghis Khan designed the campaigns in the Muslim lands to be part of a war of conquest. Massive death and destruction were the means to that end. The Mongol conquest of Khwarazm has been neatly summarized: "No city withstood their onslaught. No citadel survived untaken. No prayers could save the people. No officials could bribe or talk their way out of submission. Nothing could slow, much less stop, the Mongol juggernaut."[10]

Genghis Khan's Final Campaign

WHILE WINTERING in Afghanistan, Genghis Khan heard news of a rebellion in Xi Xia. He decided to return to Mongolia and prepare for another campaign against that land, a campaign that turned out to be his last.

As part of the agreement with Xi Xia that spared it further death and destruction, its ruler had promised to assist Genghis Khan when called upon to do so. In the spring of 1219, Genghis Khan sent a summons to Xi Xia demanding military assistance in the coming war with Khwarazm. The message stated: "You've said to me, 'I'll be your right hand.' Now the Moslems have broken my golden reins and I'm setting out to war with them. Send me your army to be my right hand." The Xi Xia response was not only rude but also seen as a challenge. Xi Xia's ruler refused to promise troops to the Mongol ambassador, and instead ordered him to relay this insulting message to Genghis Khan: "If he's not strong enough to conquer the Moslems alone, then why does he call himself Khan?" Upon hearing the response, Genghis Khan, enraged, stated to his generals, "If Heaven protects me, if I manage to tighten my golden reins on the Moslem people and return to Mongolia, then I'll see to the [Tanguts]."[1] In addition, in mid-1225 word reached Genghis Khan that Xi Xia had patched up its differences with the Jin and had formed an alliance. A Xi Xia–Jin alliance had the potential to threaten Mongol control over parts of northern China. Although the Mongols were still campaigning, especially in Russia, there was still no doubt that the Mongols controlled the lands of Central Asia and Persia. So in 1226 Genghis Khan led his main army on a campaign of extermination against Xi Xia.

In the nearly four years prior to this campaign, Genghis Khan's top lieutenants and aides had become concerned that the Khan was mellowing. He spent much of his time contemplating the future and his own mortality, and he engaged in long talks with a Daoist priest. The Great Khan was close to sixty years old and had lived a life of often-violent exertions. While the record does not suggest he was in poor health at this time, he did spend more time discussing a future that would carry on without him. Somehow word had reached the Khan of a wondrous, three-hundred-year-old, Daoist sage named Changchun who lived in China. In 1221 he sent for this priest. Changchun was not, in fact, three hundred years old but was over seventy. He traveled to Central Asia from Shandong (Confucius's birthplace) and met with the Mongol ruler in the spring of 1222.

The world conqueror and the spiritual priest held many conversations about life and death, but the Khan's first question was about a magic elixir for immortality. Changchun informed Genghis Khan that no such magic elixir existed. This was not what Genghis Khan wanted to hear, but he did not erupt in a rage or order Changchun killed. When he allowed Changchun to return to China, he issued a decree protecting Changchun and his followers and exempting them from taxation. From his talks with the Daoist, Genghis Khan gained acceptance that his time on the earth was coming to an end. Before he left this earth, however, he had some unfinished business to take care of in Xi Xia. As he prepared, he learned that Mukali had died in China. Of his greatest generals only Subodei remained, and he was then campaigning in Russia.

Before departing for Xi Xia, Genghis Khan ordered that all "unnecessary" prisoners be executed. If carried out, this edict would have led to the deaths of thousands right in the middle of the Mongol camp. His generals worried that a panic would ensue and compromise their ability to move. So, they did not fully carry out this order, but released many of the prisoners, keeping several thousand to manage their supplies and do the digging and other work the Mongols required.

The Mongol army entered Xi Xia territory in February 1226 and immediately sacked several towns and villages on the border. They were delighted to find these towns heavily stocked with food and other provisions. The army mercilessly cut down the populations, in accord with Genghis Khan's intention to punish the people of Xi Xia. As the armies moved deeper into the land, the slaughter continued. In the words of one Chinese writer at the time: "Men strive in vain to hide in caverns and in mountains. As to the Mongol sword, hardly two in a hundred escape it. The fields are covered with the bones of slaughtered people."[2] A war of extermination, not just conquest, was intended and Genghis Khan wanted as many of Xi Xia's inhabitants killed as possible. Only parts of Persia and Afghanistan suffered a similar level of devastation.

By summer 1226 the Mongols converged on the two main remaining cities, one of which was Ningxia, the capital. The Xi Xia armies had fled behind the walls of these cities. Indeed, during this campaign the Mongols rarely faced large enemy armies in the field, making Mongol progress much easier and allowing them to engage in systematic slaughter with relative lack of interference. To prevent relief forces coming from Jin China, another Mongol army under Khan's son, Ögödei, besieged the Jin capital at Kaifeng.

Over the next year the Mongols put a tight siege around Ningxia and continued the campaign of slaughter and devastation of the land. The city defended itself against several Mongol assaults, holding out as long and as furiously as it did probably because the Xi Xia's ruler believed the Mongols would eventually leave. He was almost granted his wish when Genghis Khan fell from his horse while hunting. This injury caused the Great Khan to contract a ferocious fever, and it was not clear if he would survive. His commanders suggested they lift the siege and return to Mongolia, where Genghis Khan could heal. Even though feverish, he rejected this suggestion and ordered that the campaign continue.

As it became clear that he would not survive long, Genghis Khan gave a few last instructions to his generals and advisors. The campaign against Xi Xia must be completed and the ruler, his officials, and their families completely exterminated. He also provided a plan for the final conquest of

Jin China, which, when finally executed a few years hence, succeeded. Then, in 1227 the Great Khan died. It is not known whether he lived long enough to learn that Xi Xia's ruler had offered to surrender the city of Ningxia. But he had clearly expired by the time the king and his officials showed themselves in the Mongol camp, laden with a large number of gifts and slaves. The Mongols informed the king and his entourage that they would not meet the Khan in person and were to submit outside the doorway to his tent. They did not tell the king that Genghis Khan was dead, probably out of concern that knowledge of the Great Khan's death might inspire the king to hold out longer. After allowing the Xi Xia king and his officials to deliver their gifts and prostrate themselves outside Genghis Khan's tent, the Mongols executed them all, as well as the remainder of Ningxia's population. Indeed, Genghis Khan had ordered his army to not leave even dogs and chickens alive. Once the killing frenzy over the next several days was completed, the army did, in fact, spare a number of the survivors. They were allowed to live as slaves to Genghis Khan's wife Yesui, who had attended to him in his last days.

Specially picked units of Mongol soldiers accompanied the caravan that included Genghis Khan's body back to Mongolia. Legend has it that some units went ahead to chase everyone away and kill those who did not move fast enough. Arrangements had been made to bury the Khan along the Onon River near a sacred mountain. Exactly which mountain was to be kept secret. After burying Genghis Khan, horses tramped back and forth along the ground to disguise the location of the burial plot. The slaves who had carried the body and dug the grave were killed, as were those curious—or stupid—enough to follow the caravan. The exact burial spot is still a mystery, though, from time to time, unproved claims appear professing to have found the tomb. Thus, the builder of the world's largest empire was laid to rest in a simple earthen grave rather than a grand mausoleum, which was the burial manner for most other world conquerors.

Genghis Khan left a written statement that summed up the last years of his life and what he hoped he had accomplished:

> Heaven is weary of the inordinate luxury of China. I remain in the wild region of the north; I return to the simplicity and seek moderation once more. As for the garments that I wear and the meals that I eat, I have the same rags and the same food as cowherds and

grooms, and I treat the soldiers as my brothers. In a hundred battles I have been in the forefront. Within the space of seven years I have performed a great work, and in the six directions of space everything is subject to a single rule! After us, the people of our race will wear garments of gold; they will eat sweet, greasy food, ride splendid coursers, and hold in their arms the loveliest of women, and they will forget that they owe these things to us.[3]

At the time this was written, Genghis Khan knew he had built up an empire and that this empire must eventually include all the regions of the earth. But, he also included a warning: if his successors wished to retain and expand the territories of the empire, they must adhere to the traditional Mongol way of life.

In considering the legacy of this conqueror, Genghis Khan's most remarkable achievement was to go against the steppe traditions, both social and military. Those traditions were not easy to change. The focus on merit—primarily military merit—and personal loyalty to Genghis Khan led to the destruction of traditional tribal organizations and the creation of a new Mongol nation. But tribal society did not disappear entirely, and the Mongols sought for centuries to recreate the degree of unity and power they had possessed under Genghis Khan. He had chosen his son, Ögödei, as his successor, but it took two years for that decision to be confirmed at a Kuriltay. And, after Ögödei's death in 1241, the rivalries among Genghis Khan's descendants grew eventually into war.

Impressively, unlike any steppe empire in previous history, the Mongol successors to Genghis Khan did hold on to much of the empire for several decades. Through a combination of military enforcement, clear administration, and utilization of competent local officials, the empire was stable and even prosperous after recovering from the devastations of conquest. Even more impressive, Genghis Khan's successors expanded the territories of the empire to encompass nearly the entire Middle East, Song China, eastern Europe, and even much of Southeast Asia. Just as Genghis Khan had chosen to initiate a major war against Kara-Khitai and Khwarazm while still fighting in China, his successors in the 1250s sent two major armies to conquer the rest of the Middle East and Southern Song China at the same time.

Militarily, the changes wrought by Genghis Khan were more long lasting among the Mongols than even his changes to Mongol society. This is possibly because his changes were proven to be so effective—not only in creating an empire but also in retaining much of the conquered territory as well. The Mongols retained the military system that Genghis Khan had left them. The army was comprised of a core of Mongols and other closely related nomadic tribes and supplemented by large numbers of Chinese, Khitans, Turks, and others. In addition, to better support their need for training and practice, the Mongol army was now equipped with weapons made out of the best materials available and by some of the finest craftsmen drawn from the vast reaches of the Mongol empire.

Genghis Khan's successors took to heart the emphasis he placed on planning and flexibility. The campaigns of the post-Genghis Khan period that attempted to complete the conquest of Song China and the lands of the Abbasid Caliphate were much slower, more methodically planned expeditions, and the Mongol invaders then systematically destroyed enemy armies and occupied their lands. These campaigns were very different from the lightning cavalry strikes favored by Genghis Khan. Yet Genghis Khan had recognized the trade-off in speed when utilizing Chinese and Muslim units in his armies, their siege capabilities outweighed this disadvantage, and it is likely he would have approved of the advances made by Mongol armies since his time.

The most successful of his successors—Batu (conqueror of eastern Europe), Hülegü (conqueror of the Middle East), and Khubilai (conqueror of Song China and much of the rest of East Asia)—also continued the Great Khan's policy of promotion of subordinates based on competence, experience, and/or loyalty rather than birth, wealth, or connections. It may be that Genghis Khan's ability to choose competent subordinates was just as important as his organizational abilities in explaining his success. One scholar of the Khan states, "It is no exaggeration to claim that his genius lay primarily in his talent as a general, his knowledge of men, and his ability in organization."[4] His boldness and willingness to take calculated risks must also be considered by anyone attempting to understand this man.

His successors were not nearly as faithful in following his instructions to remain true to the steppes from which they came. Genghis Khan saw cities and the "civilized" way of life as dangers to be avoided at all cost.

During Mongol conquests he rarely left behind more than small garrisons, with a few Mongols to oversee the rule (more often the plunder) of the conquered territories. For administration he relied on mostly Uighurs and Khitans, though others were used if they proved useful and loyal. Later Mongol rulers continued to rely heavily on non-Mongols and non-nomadic people to administer the empire, but then they really had no choice: the empire was much too large and complex for the few hundred thousands of Mongols to effectively administer. Compared with those during Genghis Khan's rule, the garrisons in places such as Persia and China became larger, and the Mongol leaders and officers became much more involved in the state of their domains. They increasingly came to enjoy the luxuries and other pleasures these lands could provide, and they spent less time on martial fitness and training.

Genghis Khan, the great empire builder, had shown what was possible if the Mongols remained united and followed his prescription and example. The only thing he could not provide to those who came later was another military and organizational genius like him.

Notes

Preface

1. From Ata-Malik Juvaini's *Genghis Khan: The History of the World Conqueror*, a history of the Mongol conquests, quoted in John Man, *Genghis Khan: Life, Death, and Resurrection* (New York: Thomas Dunne Books, 2004), 156.

Chapter 1

1. J. J. Saunders, *The History of the Mongol Conquests* (Philadelphia: University of Pennsylvania Press, 1971), 14, 46.
2. Paul Ratchnevsky, *Genghis Khan: His Life and Legacy*, trans. and ed. Thomas Nivison Haining (Malden, MA: Blackwell, 1991), 6–7.
3. Leo de Hartog, *Genghis Khan: Conqueror of the World* (London: I. B. Taurus, 1999), 4.
4. Saunders, *Mongol Conquests*, 45.
5. René Grousset, *The Empire of the Steppes: A History of Central Asia*, trans. Naomi Walford (New Brunswick, NJ: Rutgers University Press, 1970), 193.

Chapter 2

1. Paul Kahn, *The Secret History of the Mongols: The Origin of Chingis Khan; An Adaptation of the Yüan ch'ao pi shih, Based Primarily on the English Translation by Francis Woodman Cleaves* (Boston: Cheng & Tsui, 1998). This book was written some years after Genghis Khan's death and was most likely commissioned by his son and successor, Ögödei. It is primarily the story of the rise of Genghis Khan and the creation of his empire, and, at points, it is surprisingly critical of the Great Khan.

2. *Secret History*, quoted in Jeremiah Curtin, *The Mongols: A History* (Conshohocken, PA: Combined Books, 1996), 16–17.

3. R. P. Lister, *Genghis Khan* (New York: Cooper Square Press, 1969), 23.

4. Ratchnevsky, *Genghis Khan*, xv. Ratchnevsky suggests that stories of Genghis Khan's fear of his mother and wife were intended as insults, to imply that he was less than a full man and under the weakening influence of women.

5. Kahn, *Secret History*, 31.

6. Lister, *Genghis Khan*, 77.

Chapter 3

1. Kahn, *Secret History*, 42.

2. See Ratchnevsky, *Genghis Khan*, 37–41, for discussion of the various explanations of this incident.

3. Kahn, *Secret History*, 43–45; this passage also tells us that it was the tribal leaders who initiated the campaign for Temüjin's promotion.

4. Kahn, *Secret History*, 59–60.

5. See long description of this incident in Lister, *Genghis Khan*, 181–85. It appears Temüjin was either moved by sentimentality or concern at angering Jamuga's remaining followers, since he attempted to convince Jamuga to join him as vassal. When Jamuga refused, he was wrapped in a blanket and crushed beneath the hooves of horses.

6. Saunders, *Mongol Conquests*, 52.

Chapter 4

1. Giovanni di Plano Carpini, *The Story of the Mongols Whom We Call the Tartars*, trans. Erik Hildinger (Boston: Branden, 1996), 71. In 1245, the pope sent Carpini as an emissary to the Mongols, and he had a meeting with Guyuk, the Great Khan at the time and grandson of Genghis Khan. Carpini noted that if one man among the unit of ten fled battle, all ten would be executed.

2. Michel Hoang, *Genghis Khan*, trans. Ingrid Cranfield (London: Saqi Books, 1990), 153–54.

3. Carpini, *Story of the Mongols*, 77–78.

Chapter 5

1. James Chambers, *Genghis Khan* (Gloucestershire, England: Sutton, 1999), 51–52.

2. Kahn, *Secret History*, 139–45. The story is covered in some detail, indicating the importance of this incident to the strengthening of Genghis Khan's position among the clans and tribes of Mongolia.

3. Michael Prawdin, *The Mongol Empire: Its Rise and Legacy* (New York: Free Press, 1967), 108.

4. Prawdin, *The Mongol Empire*, 109.

5. According to Arthur Waldron's *The Great Wall of China: From History to Myth* (Cambridge: Cambridge University Press, 1990), there was no "Great Wall" at this time. However, in "The Northern Frontier," David Wright convincingly shows that in this period there was indeed a wall in the north, even if not quite as impressive as the one later built during the Ming dynasty [in David A. Graff and Robin Higham, eds., *A Military History of China* (Boulder, CO: Westview Press, 2002), 63].

6. Hoang, *Genghis Khan*, 178.

7. Kahn, *Secret History*, 147.

8. Curtin, *The Mongols*, 86.

Chapter 6

1. René Grousset, *The Empire of the Steppes*, trans. Naomi Walford (New Brunswick, NJ: Rutgers University Press, 1970), 236.

2. Grousset, *Empire of the Steppes*, 235–36.

3. Some of the discussion and theories concerning Genghis Khan's early intentions toward Khwarazm are briefly and ably reviewed in David Morgan, *The Mongols* (Cambridge, MA: Blackwell, 1990), 67–69. See also Ratchnevsky, *Genghis Khan*, 119–23, who notes that, at this point, the war in China had actually taken a turn for the worse for the Mongols, and it was not a good time to begin another major military campaign.

4. Quoted in Hoang, *Genghis Khan*, 217.

5. Kahn, *Secret History*, 156.

6. For a detailed description of the many acts of bravery on the part of the Turkish warriors, see W. Barthold, *Turkestan Down to the Mongol*

Invasion, 3rd edition, revised (Munshiram, 2002). This author notes the Mongol policy of slaughtering Turks fighting for the shah led to many unnecessarily prolonged battles and thousands more deaths on both the Mongol and Khwarazm sides.

7. Curtin, *The Mongols,* 115.
8. Ratchnevsky, *Genghis Khan,* 136–37.
9. de Hartog, *Genghis Khan,* 107.
10. Jack Weatherford, *Genghis Khan and the Making of the Modern World* (New York: Crown, 2004), 109.

Chapter 7
1. Kahn, *Secret History,* 156–57.
2. Curtin, *The Mongols,* 137.
3. Grousset, *Empire of the Steppes,* 249.
4. de Hartog, *Genghis Khan,* 17.

This bibliography is not intended to be a complete listing of all works on the life and times of Genghis Khan but to give the reader a start on some of the more important resources on the great empire builder.

One of the best sources for background history of the steppe lands and the history of the peoples who lived there remains René Grousset, *The Empire of the Steppes: A History of Central Asia*, trans. Naomi Walford (New Brunswick, NJ: Rutgers University Press, 1970). First published in 1939, Grousset's book is an excellent way to gain an understanding of the various peoples of the steppes, and the bulk of the book deals with the Mongols. Next, for primary sources one must consult *The Secret History of the Mongols*. The majority of this anonymous work (sometimes attributed to Shigi-Khutugu, Genghis Khan's adapted son) was probably composed soon after the Great Khan's death and reached final written form about 10–15 years later. Several translations are available, but one to look at is Paul Kahn's short adaptation of Francis Woodman Cleaves's translation, *The Secret History of the Mongols: The Origin of Chingis Khan* (Boston: Cheng & Tsui, 1998). If one is ambitious enough, a new, full translation of over thirteen hundred pages is available: Igor de Rachewiltz, *The Secret History of the Mongols: A Mongolian Epic Chronicle of the Thirteenth Century* (Boston: Brill, 2004).

Two sources from the Islamic world are particularly detailed in their description of Genghis Khan and his conquests. The first is J. A. Boyle's translation of Ala-al-Din Ata-Malik Juvaini, *Genghis Khan: The History of the World Conqueror* (Seattle: University of Washington Press, 1997). The second, also translated by J. A. Boyle, is Rashid al-Din Tabib, *The Successors of Genghis Khan* (New York: Columbia University Press, 1971). Juvaini published his work in 1260 and it contains valuable detail on the Mongol campaigns in the Islamic world. Rashid al-Din Tabib (a Jewish convert to Islam) was employed by the Mongol rulers of Persia to compose a comprehensive history, which he completed in 1295. He was very sensitive about how he described his Mongol masters, but was given access to the vast array of sources on the Mongol conquests then available. One somewhat contemporary European source by a papal envoy, Friar Giovanni di Plano Carpini, *The Story of the Mongols Whom We Call the Tartars*, trans. Erik Hildinger (Boston: Branden Publishing, 1996) contains a particularly good description of the Mongol lifestyle and military organization and training.

There are numerous longer secondary works on Genghis Khan and his conquests, but several stand out as particularly informative. Two general histories of the period are David Morgan, *The Mongols* (Cambridge, MA: Blackwell Publishers, 1990) and J. J. Saunders, *The History of the Mongol Conquests* (Philadelphia: University of Pennsylvania Press, 1971). It is no coincidence that both these authors are specialists in Islamic history, as most of the best primary sources on the Mongols are in Persian. Both authors also write in a very engaging, accessible style. Leo de Hartog, *Genghis Khan: Conqueror of the World* (New York: I. B. Taurus, 1999) is a very good comprehensive life of Genghis Khan. Hartog's book is only surpassed by the one book all who are interested in the life of Genghis Khan should read: Paul Ratchnevsky, *Genghis Khan: His Life and Legacy* (Malden, MA: Blackwell, 1991). In addition to his wonderful narrative history, Ratchnevsky also discusses various interpretations and controversies surrounding the history of Genghis Khan.

One of the best descriptions of the Mongol army and the strategies and tactics utilized by Genghis Khan and his generals is contained in several sections of Richard A. Gabriel, *Subotai the Valiant: Genghis Khan's Greatest General* (Westport, CT: Praeger, 2004). John Man, *Genghis Khan: Life, Death, and Resurrection* (New York: Thomas Dunne Books, 2004) offers a portrayal of Genghis Khan and his life, enlivened by the author's description of his personal travels to the many territories of the Mongol empire.

Index

About the Author

Paul Lococo, Jr., received his doctorate in Chinese military history at the University of Hawaii-Manoa and is currently associate professor of history at the Leeward College campus. His recent research and publications focus on premodern Asian military history, and he is the coauthor with Stephen Morillo and Michael Pavkovic of *War in World History: Society, Technology, and War from Ancient Times to the Present: Part IV: The Dawn of Global Warfare, 1500–1750*. He lives in Pearl City, Hawaii.